To
John B. Moreau Esq
with the kind regards
of his friend
Benson J. Lossing

July 1. 1867

Matthew Vassar

VASSAR COLLEGE

AND ITS

FOUNDER

BY BENSON J LOSSING

NEW YORK
C A ALVORD PRINTER
1867

PREFACE.

THE correspondence on another page answers all proper inquiries concerning the origin and meaning of this volume. It is right to say here, that to the generous liberality of Mr. Vassar, who gladly co-operated with the Executive Committee, the Author is indebted for the means necessary to make this work an example of great excellence in the wedded arts of Engraving and Printing.

Nearly all of the illustrations were drawn on the wood by JOHN F. RUNGE—a greater number of them from his original sketches made for the work. The Engravings, excepting the portrait of the Founder, from the burin of J. C. BUTTRE, are by LOSSING & BARRITT, and the printing by C. A. ALVORD.

The Author here records his grateful acknowledgments to the Founder, the Officers and Trustees, and the

Faculty and Teachers of Vassar College, for their kind and cheerful assistance in furnishing information for his use in the preparation of this Memoir.

POUGHKEEPSIE, N. Y.
June, 1867.

CORRESPONDENCE.

VASSAR COLLEGE,

POUGHKEEPSIE, N. Y., *March* 15, 1867.

Mr. BENSON J. LOSSING:—

DEAR SIR:—At a recent meeting of the Executive Committee of this College, the consideration of the propriety and importance of collecting and embodying the main facts in the life of Mr. Matthew Vassar, especially as connected with the foundation and establishment of this College, led to the unanimous adoption of the following preamble and resolution, which I have great pleasure in officially communicating to you:

"*Whereas*, It is desirable that the College should possess, as a matter of public interest, and as a record to be perpetually preserved, a Memoir of its Founder, Matthew Vassar, and a succinct history of the inception and final establishment of this College;

"*And whereas*, Benson J. Lossing is one of its trustees, and eminently qualified for such a labor; therefore,

"*Resolved*, That Mr. Lossing be requested to prepare, in such form and style as his judgment, experience, and taste, and the greatness of the enterprise may suggest, a History of the College, and of its Founder; and that the Founder, and all officers of the College, be requested to place at his disposal all facts and documents he may desire."

It is earnestly hoped you may be able to take the work in hand at once, and while Mr. Vassar's powers of mind and body remain so remarkably unimpaired.

Very respectfully and truly yours,

C. SWAN, *Secretary*.

POUGHKEEPSIE, N. Y., *March* 16, 1867.

DEAR SIR:—

Your note, conveying the resolution of the Executive Committee of the Board of Trustees of Vassar College, inviting me to prepare a Memoir of its Founder, and a brief history of its inception and final establishment, is received.

I accept the invitation with satisfaction, and with thanks for the expression of confidence of the Executive Committee.

I will endeavor to have the task completed before the close of the current collegiate year.

I am, very respectfully,

Your friend and co-worker,

BENSON J. LOSSING.

MR. C. SWAN,

Secretary of the Board of Trustees of Vassar College.

BIRTH-PLACE.

N a pleasant rural city on the eastern bank of the Hudson River lives a man, while this sentence is flowing from the pen, who has passed, by the space of five years, the Scripture limit of active human life. In person he is a little less than medium height, well proportioned, and compactly built. He has a fair complexion, with lingerings of the ruddiness of good health upon his cheeks. The brown hair of his earlier days is much outmeasured by the whiter crown of age. His dark gray eyes beam with the luster of vigorous middle life and the radiance of inextinguishable good-humor. His nose is of the Roman type and firmly set, and the general expression of his face is pleasant to friends and strangers; for upon his countenance, whether in action or in repose, is seen the perpetual sunshine of a gentle, cheerful nature; while his voice, low and flexible, is always musical with kindly cadences. Like Rowe's ideal—

> "Age sits with decent grace upon his visage,
> And worthily becomes his silver locks."

On the walls of his modest dwelling hang pictures of existing buildings which are a part of his personal history. One is clustered with associations of his infancy and earliest childhood; the other is hallowed as the noble offspring of his generous liberality in his serene old age. One is in the Eastern hemisphere, and the other in the Western, and are three thousand miles apart. One is a humble farm-house, not more than ten paces in length, and a single story in height, with pantiled roof and whitewashed walls, all fashioned after the model of the common dwelling of the English husbandman eighty years ago; the other is a palace of brick and freestone, five hundred feet in length, whose model was the Tuileries, the metropolitan residence of the French monarchs. One is in the rich maritime and agricultural County of Norfolk, in far eastern England, on the borders of the North Sea, and a small distance from the sweet little River Ouse; the other is in the wealthy agricultural County of Duchess, in the State of New York, near the pleasant City of Poughkeepsie, and not far from the majestic Hudson River. One is the humble birth-place and the other the stately memorial of MATTHEW VASSAR, the founder of VASSAR COLLEGE, for the education of Young Women.

In the farm-house alluded to, and delineated on the preceding page, then occupied by his parents while a family mansion was a-building, Matthew Vassar was born, on the 29th of April, 1792. That birth-place is in a beautiful section of Norfolk County, in a settlement known as East Dereham, parish of Tuddenham, and an easy day's journey from the ancient city of Norwich, where the first seed

Vassar College.

of England's immense manufacturing interest was planted by some Flemings in the time of Henry the First, more than seven hundred years ago. One of the earliest records on Mr. Vassar's memory is the impression made by the sight of the grand old cathedral in that city, built almost eight centuries ago by the followers of the conquering William of Normandy. Coeval and equally ineffaceable records were made by his three escapes from violent death before he was four years of age—one by tumbling over the head of one of his father's horses into a pebbly pond, in the rear of the cottage; another by a bull, made furious by the scarlet mantle worn by his sister while she was leading him across a field; and a third by a lunatic, who seized him by the hair and beat his tiny body cruelly with a cudgel. These incidents, and the impressions made by the soft voice of the cuckoo in the morning, the song of the nightingale in the evening, the pale light of the glow-worm in the grass, the beauty of the primrose and other flowers, are the pictures of his short English life that are still vivid in his memory.

Mr. Vassar's ancestors were from France, where the name, which is distinguished in French history, is spelled Vasseur or Le Vasseur. Such was the name of the private secretary of Lafayette, who accompanied him to this country more than forty years ago. The great-grandfather of Mr. Vassar crossed the channel that separates France and England early in the last century, and settled in Norfolk, where he engaged in tillage, and in wool culture, for which that county has always been famous. His posterity occupied the homestead, and followed the same pursuit. His grandson James married Anne Bennett, the excellent daughter of a neighboring farmer, and these were the parents of him whose history we are tracing, and who was the youngest of their four children who were born in England, and named respectively Sophia, Maria, John Guy, and Matthew.

James Vassar and his wife were Dissenters of the Baptist order, and, in common with other non-conformists, felt the oppressions of the wedded Church and State. At the time of their younger son's birth, the French Revolution was upheaving all Europe with its volcanic fires, and shaking England, politically and socially, to its deepest foundations. It vivified in the hearts of the Dissenters the spirit of Liberty, such as Milton and Sidney had cherished, and a cry for justice was heard throughout the realm. While Burke, with strange inconsistency, thundered against the French Revolution and the Reform Associations of Great Britain, making his former political friends tremble lest he should reveal their secrets, and denounce their designs, Doctors Price and Priestley, Lords Stanhope and Lauderdale, Horne Tooke, Thelwall, and others, gave the citadel of Privilege such heavy blows with the weapons of Reason, strong in Christian ethics, that even the Throne was made to tremble. Then the Church and State, made cruel by fear, resolved to stamp into the earth the vigorous plant of Democracy, that threatened to overrun their domain. With their enormous wealth and influence, and long retinue of retainers, they put forth their strength in the form of Law, and violated justice by prosecutions for political *designs* rather than for political *offenses*, and in transporting men to a penal colony for seven and fourteen years, whose crimes consisted chiefly in having read Paine's *Rights of Man* and expressed partial approbation of its doctrines!

The Crown and the Mitre were too strong for the Tribune and the Conventicle, and their threatenings, as in the days of the First Charles, drove many of the best subjects of the Empire across the Atlantic, in search of that civil and religious liberty which their unnatural Mother denied them. On the tombs of many of those emigrants might have been justly written words similar to those sent over by William Roscoe, the English poet, to be inscribed on the white marble slab that now stands at the grave of his friend John Taylor (one of the emigrants), in Christ Church Cemetery in Poughkeepsie. Roscoe wrote—

"Far from his country and his native skies,
Here, mouldering in the dust, poor TAYLOR lies.
Firm was his mind, and fraught with various lore;
And his warm heart was never cold before.
He loved his country—loved that spot of earth
Which gave a MILTON, HAMPDEN, BRADSHAW birth;
But when that country, dead to all but gain,
Bowed its base neck and hugged th' Oppressor's chain,
Loathing the abject scene, he drooped, he sighed,

Crossed the wild wave, and here untimely died.
Stranger, whate'er thy country's Creed, or Hue,
Go, and like him the moral path pursue;
Go, and for Freedom every peril brave,
And nobly scorn to be or hold a slave."

It was in that exodus, and in the year 1796, that James Vassar and his wife and children, with his bachelor brother, Thomas, came to the United States in search of liberty of conscience. They were the first of their name on this side of the Atlantic. With many sighs they left their birth-land they loved so well. An Englishman's loyalty may seldom be justly questioned, for Home is his ideal of Heaven, and his heart always turns lovingly toward his native land, as the blossom of the heliotrope turns toward the sun.

It was in the ship *Criterion*, Captain Samuel Avery, that the Vassar family left the port of London, and, after a boisterous voyage, arrived in the harbor of New York on a beautiful day in October, in good health and spirits. A wave that broke over the vessel during a gale, had swept Matthew from the cabin gangway across the deck, and he was saved from the sea only by the net-work of the taffrail. But the perils of the Atlantic were passed in safety by the whole family, and they found comfortable quarters in New York in the house of an Englishman named Withington, the owner of an extensive brewery in the suburbs of the city.

New York had then a population of about fifty thousand souls. The people were agitated by great political excitement, the leaven of French democracy being the chief cause. It was on the eve of a Presidential Election. Washington's second administration was drawing to a close. His Farewell Address to his countrymen, warning them against the dangers of foreign influence, had just been scattered broadcast through the public press. The nation was called upon to choose a new Executive head. Adams and Jefferson were the opposing aspirants for that lofty position. The ardent friends of Jefferson were seen in the streets with the flaunting tricolored cockade of the French Revolution on their hats, while those of Adams wore the modest black cockade of the American Revolution. The fierce struggle of the *Federal* and *Democratic* parties for supremacy was at its height; and, to the apprehension of the newly arrived Englishmen, a terrible revolution was at hand. They heard the Government openly denounced and menaced, yet its strong arm was still, and it seemed powerless to save itself. And their hearts were troubled when they heard ribald voices chanting the National air of England burdened with these terrible words:—

"God save the Guillotine!
Till England's King and Queen
Its power shall prove;
Till each anointed knob
Affords a clipping job,
Let no rude halter rob
The Guillotine!"

But that election left society quiet and the government secure at its close; and satisfied the immigrants that they were in a land of liberty indeed; that freedom of thought, and speech, and action, was not only their privilege but their right; and that there was absolute safety where Conscience was untrammeled, and Reason was left free to combat Error. With this conviction, they sought a permanent home in the proposed land of their adoption.

At that time the fertile Mohawk Valley, in the State of New York, was a point of great attraction to agriculturists, and it was rapidly filling up with settlers. General Schuyler, Elkanah Watson, Christopher Colles, and other far-seeing men, had projected a canal that should traverse that Valley, and connect the waters of Lake Erie with those of the Hudson River. That project, if carried out, promised great advantages to the settlers. Thither the Vassar brothers went, on a tour of observation, at the beginning of December; and traveled as far westward as Utica, the site of old Fort Schuyler, then a flourishing village of about one thousand souls. They had frequently diverged from the Mohawk Valley turnpike, the main line of travel, to examine the country. Much of it was just emerging from the wilderness state, and presented a positive contrast to the beauty, order, and cultivation of their beloved England. It was covered with snow, and was most dreary in every aspect; and the brothers returned to New York late in January, so dissatisfied that they felt inclined to go back to their native land. That inclination was almost a fixed purpose, when the fertility and pleasant features of Duchess County, in the same State, were brought to their notice by one or two English families who were about to settle there, and early in the Spring of 1797 the brothers went with them to Poughkeepsie, then an unincorporated village of a few hundred souls.

This was more than ten years before Fulton achieved his triumph in navigation, in the crude steamer *Clermont*, and the Vassar brothers made the voyage in a packet sloop, then the only mode of travel on the river. They explored the country about Poughkeepsie, and finally purchased a farm, containing about one hundred and fifty acres, in the rich and beautiful valley of the Wappengi's Creek, about three miles eastward of the village, on the verge of which a cotton-factory (now a paper-mill), and hamlet of workmen, named Manchester, were afterwards built by the late Samuel Slee, who was also an Englishman.

Soon after their purchase, James took his family to Poughkeepsie, and while he was preparing a dwelling on the farm, they occupied a brick house about a mile east of the village, on the Filkintown road, at what is now the junction of Main and Church Streets. That was Matthew Vassar's first place of residence in Poughkeepsie. It fell into ruins a few years

MR. VASSAR'S FIRST RESIDENCE IN POUGHKEEPSIE.

ago, and when in that state it was painted for Mr. Vassar by F. Rondel, from whose picture the annexed sketch is made.

At the close of the summer the farm-house was finished, and the whole family were in it, happy in finding rest after a year of wandering. That broad valley reminded them of the fields they had left in Norfolk. The stream that washed its borders seemed like the little rivers of their native land; and when, in the Autumn, the fertile soil gave back to them a bountiful return for labor, they were contented.

The creek that bears the name of the Wappengi tribe of Mohegan Indians, who dwelt at its falls near the Hudson two hundred years ago, and traverses Duchess County from northeast to southwest, about forty miles, is everywhere a picturesque stream; but at no point was it more lovely than along the plain of Manchester, at the time we are considering, when stately sycamores with their huge and ghostly stems stood by its margin, their majesty disputing for the prize of admiration with the beauty of the elms that spread high in air their graceful tops, while the modest willow hung lovingly over the nourishing waters. More modest still, the dog-

The Wappengi's Creek.

wood, with its white blossoms in early Spring; the alder with its dull purple catkins, and the witch-hazel and the elder, made up the more humble curtains of stem and leaf that everywhere half concealed the stream. But to the eyes of the English settlers nothing was more pleasing than a score of saplings along the borders of their farm, draped with the spiral vines of the wild hop (*humulus lupulus*), from whose clustering blossoms they might distill the lupuline for home-brewed ale, without which an English family would experience a real privation. But barley for the malt was lacking. It was not long a want; for when the farm-work was over in the Autumn, Thomas went to England for a supply of that grain and other cereals, and of good sheep. He brought back with him some fine seed rath, the most profitable kind of barley for brewing; and in the Summer of 1798, the first field of that grain ever seen in Duchess County ripened and yielded bountifully on the Vassar farm, in the valley of the Wappengi. There it was that the mournful drama of John Barley-corn and the three kings, so sadly told by young Burns, was first performed within the bounds of the ancient shire, when

They laid him down upon his back
 And cudgeled him full sore;
They hung him up before the storm,
 And turned him o'er and o'er.

They fillèd up a darksome pit
 With water to the brim;
They heavèd in John Barley-corn—
 There let him sink or swim.

They laid him out upon the floor
 To work him farther woe;
And still, as signs of life appeared,
 They tossed him to and fro.

They wasted o'er a scorching flame
 The marrow of his bones;
But a miller used him worst of all,
 For he crushed him 'tween two stones.

But the woe of John wrought joy in the family of James, for when apples were ripening in September, there was home-brewed ale in his house. The fame of it was soon spread abroad among the thirsty neighbors. The thrifty family made it for sale; and it was not long before little Matthew and his mother might occasionally be seen on the road to Poughkeepsie, in the farm wagon, with a barrel of home-brewed ale, the freshest eggs, and the yellowest butter, for all of which an ever-ready market was found.

So general became the demand for Vassar's ale, that in the year 1801 the brothers sold their farm, and James began the business of brewing in Poughkeepsie, which was incorporated a village that year. He purchased a lot of land of the heirs of Baltus Van Kleeck, lying between the Upper Landing road (now Mill Street) and the new road then just opened to the river, in continuation of what is now Main Street, west from Washington Street. On that lot he built a brewery, and in a part of it his family dwelt while he was erecting the house in which the founder of Vassar College now resides.

Adjoining the Vassar lot on the Upper Landing road, and a few rods east of the present Vassar Street, stood the venerable homestead of the Van Kleeck family. It was built of rough stone, in the year 1702, by Baltus Van Kleeck, one of the earlier of the immigrants from Holland who settled in Duchess County toward the close of the seventeenth century. It was the first substantial house built on the site of Poughkeepsie. In its gables, and just under its eaves, the walls were pierced with loop-holes for musketry, for at that time the Indians were numerous in the county, and were feared by the settlers. Van Kleeck's house was a sort of citadel for the hamlet of Poughkeepsie, in which the score or two of its inhabitants might take refuge. The lintel of the main door was a rough-hewn stone from the fields, on which were cut the date of erection, and the initials of the name of the owner, in duplicate. That lintel is now a corner-stone, close to the pavement, of the dwelling of Matthew Vassar, Jr., who is a lineal descendant of Van

STONE LINTEL.

Kleeck, his father, John Guy, the elder brother of the Founder, having married Margaret, a daughter of Baltus Van Kleeck, and a great-granddaughter of the first-named Baltus.

That old mansion was well filled with good furniture brought from Holland, some of which is in the possession of M. Vassar, Jr. An immense round table of mahogany, a high-backed sofa and chairs, are among the remnants of it, and afford good specimens of the equipment—*huys-raedt*—of a Hollandsche family of the better sort, for house-keeping. But more precious things than the most costly furniture were seen in that old mansion. These were Patriots —men such as Sir William Jones made Alcæus of Mitylene declare were the constituents of a State:

SOFA.

> "Men, who their duties know,
> But know their rights, and knowing dare maintain;
> Prevent the long-aimed blow,
> And crush the tyrant while they rend the chain."

That house, then a public inn, was a place of resort for the Patriots of the neighborhood for many miles around, during the whole period of the old War for Independence. There they met for consultation after the Boston Port Bill had blasted all hope of reconciliation between the colonists and the British Ministry on a basis of justice. There the Committee of Correspondence for Duchess County, with Egbert Benson at its head, held meetings. There, in June and July, 1775, the Whigs of "Poughkeepsie Precinct" signed a pledge, "under all the ties of religion, honor, and love of country," to sustain whatever measures the Continental Congress and the Provincial Convention of New York should resolve upon for preserving the liberties of the people. There the Legislature of the State of New York assembled, early in 1778 (the Court-house being in ruins), after having fled from Kingston on the approach of the British incendiaries under

THE VAN KLEECK HOUSE.

General Vaughan, who burned that village at the middle of the preceding Autumn; and there, a little more than ten years later, Hamilton, Jay, Hobart, Duane, Yates, Clinton, Livingston, Bancker, Van Cortlandt, and other distinguished men, may have found lodgings (it being the only inn in the village), while sojourning more than a month in Poughkeepsie, in the Summer of 1788, as members of the State Convention that sat in the new Court-house to consider the ratification of the National Constitution.

That old "Van Kleeck House" was thus made famous by the presence of famous men. It was strong enough to resist the busy fingers of decay for centuries; but, like many another building in our changeful land, hallowed by events that touch the sympathies of our higher nature, it was compelled to give place to more modern structures. It came into the possession of the Vassar family by inheritance, and so it remained until 1835, when it was pulled down, but not until its features had been preserved by the pencil of the writer of this Memoir.

James Vassar was successful as a brewer, and he contemplated making his two sons his assistants. John Guy was between two and three years the senior of Matthew, and was useful to his father from the beginning. But, when his younger brother was old enough to take a part in the business, the latter evinced so great an aversion to it, that his father made an arrangement to apprentice him for seven years to a tanner in Poughkeepsie. This was a business still more distasteful to the boy than brewing. He vehemently protested, but in vain. Articles of indenture were drawn; and on a specified morning he was to enter the service of a legal master. When that time arrived, the lad was not to be found. He had appealed to his mother, and excited her active sympathy in his distress. He had begged to be allowed to go out into the world to "seek his fortune," as the phrase is, alone, and she resolved that he should do so. With a change of East India muslin shirts and a pair of stockings tied up in a cotton bandanna handkerchief (which, with a homespun suit, woolen stockings, stout shoes, and a cap, in which he was clad, composed his entire wardrobe), he left his home on a pleasant morning in the Spring of 1806, accompanied by his mother. They walked to the New Hamburg ferry, eight miles below Poughkeepsie, and there they parted. After giving him her blessing, and a cash capital of seventy-five cents, the mother lingered in tears on the bank of the stream, until she saw her child in safety on the opposite shore, and a river half a mile wide between the tanner and the boy.

Young Vassar was now fairly out upon a business

journey on his own account. He walked on toward Newburgh in search of employment, when, toward evening, his weariness emboldened him to ask a farmer, who was passing by in his wagon, to allow him to ride. The man was somewhat rough in speech, and accused him of being a runaway. The lad gave him his name and a truthful account of what had happened, when the farmer, who was a kind-hearted Englishman named Butterworth, told the boy that he knew his father, and then invited the wanderer to lodge at his house that night. It was near a little settlement two miles north of Newburgh, called Balm Town, where Butterworth's son had a country store.

On the following morning, young Vassar made a bargain with the merchant to perform the drudgery in his store. His diligence, integrity, and intelligence soon caused his promotion. On the basis of a very limited education, he there laid the foundations of a business ability excelled in efficiency by few men. He remained with Butterworth about three years, and then entered the store of Daniel Smith, another merchant, as first clerk, at the then considerable salary of three hundred dollars annually. There he served faithfully about twelve months, when he returned home, after an absence of four years, with one hundred and fifty dollars saved from his earnings in "foreign service," as he termed it. Then he entered his father's flourishing establishment as book-keeper and collector.

A year later the elder Vassar was smitten by heavy misfortunes. On the 10th of May, 1811, while he was going up the Hudson on a sloop, he saw flames and a heavy smoke at Poughkeepsie that told of a conflagration. He felt a presentiment that it was his own property; and it was. His brewery, on which he had no insurance, was in flames, and it was utterly consumed. That "misfortunes seldom come single," is a popular saying and belief. It was verified in Mr. Vassar's experience. Two days after his property was destroyed, his son John Guy, then twenty-two years of age, lost his life by descending into a recently emptied beer-vat amidst the ruins, in which were some hops that might be saved. It was charged with carbonic acid gas, and he was

Anne Vassar.

James Vassar.

suffocated. Other losses of property followed; and when they were past fifty years of age, James Vassar and his wife found themselves with a large family of children, reduced to comparative poverty. Business efforts failed; and the future appeared gloomy and utterly unpromising to the almost disheartened man. Finally, he leased and closely tilled fourteen acres of land on the New York and Albany post-road, a little north of the Fall Kil, in the suburbs of Poughkeepsie; and there, in a quaint old house, on the site of the present residence of Stephen M. Buckingham, he and his wife passed a greater part of the evening of their lives in comfort and serenity. Mrs. Vassar died in March, 1837, and her husband survived her only three years.

James Vassar's brother Thomas, who came with him to America, and was his partner in the farm on the Wappengi's Creek, established himself in the business of brick-making, two miles east of Poughkeepsie, soon after he left the valley of the Wappengi, and continued it until within a few years of his death, which occurred in October, 1849, when he was almost ninety-three years of age. His wife, Joanna Ellison, who was twenty years his junior, lived three years longer. The remains of these worthy people—the ancestors of the Vassar family in this country—who left their birthland for the sake of liberty of conscience, were all laid in the Baptist Cemetery near the banks of the Fall Kil, or the Winnakee, as the Indians more sweetly named it. This is a small stream that flows through Poughkeepsie, and falls in a series of cascades into what was once a sheltered cove of the Hudson, which the aborigines called Apokeepsing, or Safe Harbor, from which the beautiful rural city on its borders derives its name.

THOMAS VASSAR.

The misfortunes of his family made Matthew Vassar more thoughtful and diligent than ever. He considered how he should employ his limited experience in brewing so as to make it profitable to himself and a comfort to his parents. Small means were at hand, and he used them with success. In a dye-house belonging to George Booth, the husband of his sister Maria, who was engaged in the manufacture of woolen cloth in Poughkeepsie, he began the business of ale-making on a scale almost as humble as did "Willie," who only

—"brewed a peck o' maut."

With a few kettles and tubes he made ale at the rate of three barrels at a time, which he sold to the citizens in small

THE COURT-HOUSE.

quantities, and delivered it with his own hands; and in the Spring of 1812 he hired a basement room in the County Court-house, which was "an elegant and substantial edifice of stone," erected in 1809, on the corner of Main and Market Streets, in which he opened a shop for the sale of Ale and Oysters. This was the first "oyster saloon" established in the town. All day long Mr. Vassar might have been seen brewing at the dye-house, or going about the village with his ale, or disposing of his "grains," as the barley was popularly called after it had served the purpose of brewing; while his evenings, until midnight, were devoted to his customers in his "saloon."

Mr. Vassar had faith in the assertion of the Sacred Proverbialist, that he who is "diligent in his business shall stand before kings; he shall not stand before mean men;" and he showed his faith by his works. Thrift rewarded his laborious industry. He felt a laudable desire for wealth,

"Not for to hide it in a hedge,
Nor for a train attendant,
But for the glorious privilege
Of being independent."

His field of effort was daily widening. The village which was to be his life-long home was growing rapidly. It then had a population of about three thousand souls, and contained almost five hundred dwellings and buildings for business. Eight sloops were continually employed, while the river was free of ice, in freighting from its four wharves. To the Reformed Dutch Church edifice, on the East Lane or Filkintown Road (now Main Street), that stood on the lot No. 257, now owned by Henry Myers, and that of Christ Church, on Main (now Market) Street, when the village was incorporated, eleven years before, three other church edifices had been added. An Academy had recently been built on Cannon Street, near its intersection by the present Academy Street. Two newspapers (*Poughkeepsie Journal* and *Republican Herald*) were well sustained; and the book-store of Paraclete Potter (now Archibald Wilson's) was a favorite place of resort of the educated men and women of the village and its vicinity, and of the leading politicians of the old Federal school. "The Hotel" (now Rutser's) had lately been built, and was described as "elegant and spacious;" and "five serpentine roads" connected the village on the high plain with the river, half a mile distant.

Such was Poughkeepsie when, in the year 1812, Mr. Vassar

commenced in it that business in which he was engaged for more than half a century, and earned the large fortune, one-half of which he dedicated to the vitally important work of thoroughly educating Woman.

So promising of success was Mr. Vassar's Ale and Oyster business, that he ventured to set up a domestic establishment early in the Spring of 1813, when he was not quite twenty-one years of age. On the 7th of March he and Miss Catharine Valentine were united in marriage; and in that state they lived together a few weeks less than fifty years. He hired part of a dwelling at the rate of forty dollars a year, payable in advance, which his prudent father thought was a very extravagant beginning; and the whole outfit of the young couple for housekeeping did not exceed, in cost, one hundred and fifty dollars. Yet it was a genteel display of home comforts, for the time. Neatness and industry characterized his chosen helpmate, and their humble dwelling-place had an air of elegance which more spacious mansions and more costly furnishings do not always present. With mutual interests they worked lovingly together; and, with the heritage of an Englishman's delight in domestic comforts, his heart was often full of that sweet content shadowed in Benjamin's words—

"O, the atmosphere of Home! how bright
It floats around us when we sit together
Under a bower of vine in Summer weather,
Or round the hearth-stone on a winter's night!"

The land was now full of trouble. There was war between the country of Mr. Vassar's nativity and that of his adoption. A long-gathering storm was in full career, and its disturbing energies were felt in every part of the Republic. The fife and drum were heard in every hamlet; and the flag of the recruiting sergeant was everywhere flaunted before the eyes of the abettors of "Madison's wicked war" and the opposing "blue-light and black-cockade Federalists," to the infinite delight of the one, and the insufferable disgust of the other. Everybody was a politician with decided views, and everybody indulged in decided expressions of them. There was a perpetual war of opinion in families, and in communities; and at places of public resort battles of tongues often waxed hot, and sometimes alarming to good order and propriety. Mr. Vassar's saloon was one of these arenas wherein the wordy gladiators wrestled. It had grown from a plain "oyster cellar" into quite a respectable "club-house;" and occupied three rooms in the basement of the Court-house and one on the floor above. There judges and jurors, lawyers and clients, dined and supped during the sessions of the courts. These supper parties indulged in intellectual exchange and convivial pleasures; and during the War it was often resonant with the appropriate songs of the day, when some enthusiastic vocalist, inspired by the public turmoil or the blood of John Barley-corn, could not keep his patriotism silent. So it was that after the village had been illuminated because of Perry's victory on Lake Erie, the ear was greeted with the stirring words—

"Let each man round the board bid his children remember,
With a generous expansion of soul,
The glory that plays round the Tenth of September,
And crown the return with a bowl.
Then the goblet shall foam, blow the wind high or low,
And the heart be it mournful or merry;
And the purest of wine to the mem'ry shall flow
Of the virtues and valor of Perry."

And when, a year later, the victory of Macomb and Macdonough over the forces of Governor Prevost of Canada, at

Plattsburg, made the inhabitants of menaced New York grateful for deliverance, Michael Hawkins' imitation of Negro minstrelsy—the first on record—descriptive of the event, and sung to the air of "Boyne Water," provoked unbounded merriment. To those familiar with the boastful spirit of Prevost on his invading march, and the ridiculous spectacle exhibited by his hasty retreat, especially funny seemed the concluding verse:

"Prevost scare so, he lef all behine,
Powder, ball, cannon, tea-pot, and kittle;
Some say he cotch a cold—trouble in he mine,
'Cause he eat so much raw and cole vittle.
Uncle Sam berry sorry
To be sure for he pain;
Wish he nuss heself up well an' hearty,
For General Macomb
An' Massa 'Donough home
When he notion for anudder tea-party."

Mr. Vassar came near being a soldier in arms. He had joined a volunteer company of Fusileers in time of peace, and was a member of the staff of the late Major-General John Brush at the period we are considering. At the time of the British invasion from Canada, which ended at Plattsburg, a land and naval force was menacing the city of New York, the project of the British ministry in 1777, for separating New England from the other States by seizing and holding the line of the Hudson River, having been revived. There was wide-spread alarm. Governor Tompkins ordered the militia and drafted men of the State, who had not yet taken the field, to hasten to the menaced metropolis, where citizens of every calling—

"Plumbers, founders, dyers; tinners, turners, shavers;
Sweepers, clerks, and criers; jewelers, engravers;
Clothiers, drapers, players; cartmen, hatters, tailors;
Gaugers, sealers, weighers; carpenters and sailors,"

were engaged night and day in casting up intrenchments on the heights of Brooklyn and Harlem, many of them singing the stirring words of Woodworth, inspired by the scene—

"Johnny Bull, beware! keep at proper distance,
Else we'll make you stare at our firm resistance.
Let alone the lads who are freedom tasting;
Recollect, our dads gave you once a basting.
Pickaxe, shovel, spade, crowbar, hoe, and barrow;
Better not invade; Yankees have the marrow."

The militia and levies of Duchess were summoned away, but Mr. Vassar, claiming the right to withhold services when privileges are denied, did not go. At a previous election he had been challenged when he offered his vote, and its reception had been denied on the plea that he was a native of England, and therefore an alien. Believing the same plea to be valid in his own favor when called upon to do military duty, he successfully interposed it; and he was spared the

Brewery on Vassar Street.

fatigue and losses of an inglorious campaign at Harlem, and the time so important to him in his business, for he was then engaged in the erection of the extensive brewery, the main building of which is yet standing on Vassar Street. Yet he did not withhold all service, for, with hundreds of other citizens of Poughkeepsie and vicinity, he went to the neighboring woods and swamps to collect materials for fascines, which were sent down the river in sloop-loads, to be used for gabions and other basket-work in the erection of fortifications at Brooklyn and Harlem.

Mr. Vassar had now struggled on in business about two years, alone, unaided by influential or wealthy friends, and relying solely upon his own resources, under Providence, for final success. It had often been a most severe struggle, in which he was several times nearly vanquished. Ambitious of excelling in whatever he undertook, he spared no pains or expense in the manufacture of his ale, but for want of capital to enlarge his facilities, it was made in quantity too limited to give him much profit. Capital was his great need, and in due time it came to help him.

In the Spring of 1814, Thomas Purser, an Englishman of considerable fortune, and also of some experience in brewing, who had quaffed many a mug of ale at Vassar's rooms with great satisfaction, offered himself as a partner, and also the requisite capital for carrying on the business on an extensive scale. The offer was accepted. The partnership was formed with the name of M. Vassar & Co., and the brewing and malting buildings, which extended from Vassar to Bridge Streets, were erected during the ensuing Summer. The business at the club-rooms in the Court-house was abandoned by its founder, and his whole time and attention were given to the manufacture of ale. That vocation was successful; but, owing to the failing health of Mr. Purser, the partnership lasted only about two years, when he withdrew.

Mr. Purser's place was supplied by Nathan and Mulford Conklin, then carrying on an extensive mercantile business in Poughkeepsie, and they remained in partnership with Mr. Vassar until 1829, when he purchased their interest. During that period, and a little beyond, Mr. Vassar experienced many vicissitudes in business, and, on two or three occasions, losses by fire and flood brought him to the verge of bankruptcy. But perseverance was one of the cardinal virtues of his character, and he always kept it vigorous by judicious use. With it he overcame all obstacles; and at length, when he had been engaged in brewing for about twenty years, a tide of uninterrupted prosperity bore him on to the possession of a large fortune. His business became too large to allow him to manage it well alone, and in 1832 he took in his nephews, Matthew Vassar, Jr., and John Guy Vassar, sons of his deceased brother John Guy. They were energetic, industrious, and faithful young men, and materially assisted their uncle in the enlargement of the business and profits of the establishment.

The brewery on Vassar Street soon became too limited in capacity for the increasing operations of the firm, and in 1836 a more extensive establishment, built of brick, was erected on the bank of the river, just above the Main Street Landing, where the manufacture of ale is still carried on under the original name of M. Vassar & Co. At various periods Mr. Vassar brought into the business, as partners, his brother James, James V. Harbottle, Alfred R. Booth, John Guy Vassar, 2d, Erastus Reeve, J. L. D. Lyon, and Oliver H. Booth. In May, 1866, the latter, who is one of Mr. Vassar's nephews, purchased the interest of his uncle, when the business connection of the founder of the establishment ended.

After managing his affairs diligently for more than thirty years, and becoming the possessor of a large fortune, Mr. Vassar determined to gratify a long-cherished desire by visiting Great Britain and the continent of Europe. He wished to engage less closely in business thereafter, and he resolved to make that the occasion for casting the burdens of its cares upon the younger men, his kinsmen, who were

BREWERY ON THE RIVER.

his partners. He accordingly made arrangements for himself and wife to go abroad and be absent from the country about three years. They were childless; and nothing in their domestic arrangements made it necessary for them to hasten back.

The classic prescription for the number of a dinner-party was, Not less than the Graces, nor more than the Muses. The minimum is the best number for a traveling party in civilized lands, and to that Mr. Vassar made his own conform by inviting Cyrus Swan to become the traveling companion of himself and wife. Mr. Swan was a young man of taste and observation, well informed and cultivated, genial and sympathetic. He had lately completed his preparatory studies for entering upon the practice of the Law as a vocation. In that profession, and while he was yet a student, he had rendered services which won for him the cordial esteem and confidence of Mr. Vassar; and the friendship then formed has remained unbroken.

Mr. Swan gladly accepted Mr. Vassar's generous invitation, and at the close of April, 1845, the little traveling party sailed from New York in the packet-ship *Northumberland*, Captain Griswold, bound for England. She had less than twenty passengers, among whom were the late Judge William Kent and his wife. The ship was stanch and well appointed, and was one of the largest of the sailing packets of that time. The day was bright and serene when they passed the Narrows, whose shores are guarded by great guns within strong walls, and went out upon the ocean. Every thing promised delight to the novices in marine experience; but, before the sun disappeared behind the dim purple outlines of the Navisink Hills, the never-ceasing motion of the bosom of the sea made them doubters. The inevitable sea-sickness followed; and during a voyage of twenty days they had the usual experience of

——"the monotony
Of an Atlantic trip—
Sometimes you ship a sea,
And sometimes see a ship!"

The passengers first saw land again one bright morning late in May, when The Needles, sculptured by the waves at the westernmost extremity of the Isle of Wight, were seen glittering in the sun-light. On the same day the *Northumberland* was anchored in the fine harbor of Portsmouth, under the guns of the vast fortifications of that seaport. There the travelers landed, and passed a few days in visiting the wonders of that greatest of England's naval stations.

Among these, which none but the eyes of Englishmen are supposed to be permitted to see, was the immense Naval Bakery. To this Mr. Vassar and his party gained admission by his acting in strict conformity to the maxim of the British Crown concerning its subjects, namely, *Once an Englishman always an Englishman.* In accordance with the spirit of this maxim, British cruisers impressed Anglo-American seamen into the Royal naval service; and chiefly on that account the two nations went to war, more than fifty years ago, and, after gallant fighting on both sides for thirty months, Great Britain still adhered to the maxim, and has never abandoned it. So, honestly abiding by her rule, and registering his name,—"M. Vassar, East Dereham, Tuddenham, Norfolk County,"—the place of his birth—the *Once an Englishman always an Englishman*, and his family, peered with their American eyes into all the secrets of England's great Naval Bakery.

From Portsmouth Mr. Vassar and his companions passed over to the Isle of Wight—the "divorced land" of the ancient Britons—which Cedric the Saxon colonized with Jutes and his own countrymen almost a thousand years before Columbus discovered America. Our travelers landed at Ryde. It was now the beginning of June, and that island—the loveliest of England's possessions—was glorying in the wealth of its verdure and blossoms. There every sense was regaled with the realities of all that painter and poet have delineated in pictures of English rural scenery and rural life, even to the gipsies, who in a popular ditty have been made to sing—

"All day we round the country tramp;
The birds bear not a lighter heart;
And then at night we pitch our camp,
Or soundly sleep beneath the cart.

What care we for the night-dew damp!
We pay no rent when we depart;
And like the lark we early rise—
Our clock's a Gipsy's opening eyes!"

After visiting every part of that charming island, enjoying the delights of its present beauties, and the contemplation of its feudal remains, Mr. Vassar proposed to tarry a little in Southampton before going up to London. They had been impressed with the realities of the past in visiting Carisbrooke Castle, near Newport, which is supposed to have been founded before the Roman invasion, but which was not completed until the time of Elizabeth. It is chiefly famous as the place of confinement of Charles the First, after his removal from Hampton Court; and the attention of our travelers was directed to a window, out of which, it is said, the king attempted to escape.

Leaving these remains of a darker age and a ruder civilization behind them, with a desire to commune more particularly with the present, Mr. Vassar and his companions crossed over to Southampton, one of the most bustling and important of the maritime towns of England. There they passed several days in visiting objects of special interest, such as the Free Grammar School founded by Edward the Sixth, and the Hospital established in the reign of Henry the Third. They also visited interesting places in the vicinity of the city, among which were the ruins of Calshot Castle, and Netley Abbey, situated on opposite shores of the beautiful Southampton Water.

From the busy city on the seaboard the travelers went up to London by railway, where they remained about three weeks. Mr. Vassar was then fifty-three years of age, and in the full vigor of the most robust health. He was the impersonation of perpetual activity. From early morning until late in the evening he was busy in observations of men and things. No place of note in that great city escaped his vision, and no details of institutions and business establishments that he visited were free from his scrutiny. "No man," says Mr. Swan, in a note to the author, "ever saw more and absorbed more in the same space of time. Always an early riser, always in motion, and always inquisitive; challenging every thing for its reason for being at all, and especially for being as he found it, he satisfied himself concerning the why and the wherefore of a multitude of objects and interests which the superficial observer would neither perceive nor understand." Every thing interested him; but most of all was he impressed by the great Hospital on St. Thomas Street, erected and endowed by Thomas Guy, whose family and Vassar's are connected by ties of consanguinity. That noble fruit of his kinsman's liberality is one of the most useful of England's monuments which perpetuate the memory of her distinguished men; and in the contemplation of it, the thought conceived by his visit to the Free Grammar School and the Hospital at Southampton developed in the mind of Mr. Vassar a fixed resolution to devote a large portion of his own fortune to the welfare of his fellow-men.

Thomas Guy was a native of London, where he was born about the year 1643. At the age of seventeen years he was apprenticed to a bookseller in his native city, and when he attained to his majority he began the same business on his own account, upon a capital of one thousand dollars. He established a lucrative business in the importation of Bibles from Holland, and afterwards made a profitable contract for the sale of those printed at the Oxford University in England. Very parsimonious in his habits, he soon accumulated a large fortune. He had a favorite servant girl, who was sensible and comely, and he offered her his hand in marriage. It was accepted; but, because of some trifling offense, he broke his engagement, dismissed her from his service, and lived a celibate, devoting nearly his whole time to the business of accumulating wealth, with the intention of finally using it for some benevolent object.

During the wars in Queen Anne's reign, Guy made large sums by the purchase of government securities from individuals at a depreciated rate, especially seamen's prize-tickets. He was also a fortunate dealer in stocks of the companies which were organized by speculators, without real foundations, from the years 1710 to 1719, inclusive, and especially of that known as the *South Sea Company*, incorporated in 1716, in whose bonds almost every wealthy person in England became a dealer. The shares going rapidly from the par value of one hundred pounds sterling to one thousand pounds, made many apparently very rich; and the most extravagant displays of equipages, and other evidences of wealth, were indulged in by those who, but a few months before, were poor and obscure. Guy might have been seen almost daily among the infatuated crowd of both sexes, in Exchange Alley, buying and selling those bonds. He knew their real worthlessness, and was one of a few wise ones who said, in effect,

"Five hundred millions, notes and bonds,
  Our stocks are worth in value;
But neither lie in goods or lands
  Or money, let me tell you.
Yet though our foreign trade is lost,
  Of mighty wealth we vapor,
When all the riches that we boast
  Consist of scraps of paper."

Guy operated shrewdly, and when the "South Sea Bubble," as it was called, burst, in 1720, and thousands of families in

England were impoverished, he was without the worthless bonds, and the possessor of immense wealth. He was then nearly seventy-seven years of age, and felt that it was high time for him to set about the final disposition of his entire estate. He had no near kinsfolk, and it was to be mostly devoted to some public object. He had already been a liberal contributor to the funds of St. Thomas's Hospital, situated within the area of the old manor of Southwark, and which was founded in 1213. In 1707, he caused one of its buildings to be erected at his sole expense; and he was one of its governors for many years. He was disposed to give all of his property to that institution, for the enlargement of its means for usefulness, but his friends persuaded him to found a new hospital. He purchased from the governors of St. Thomas's the lease of a lot for nine hundred and ninety-nine years; and in 1721 he caused the old buildings that occupied a portion of it to be removed. In the following spring the foundations for a hospital were laid; and at the time of his death, at the middle of December, 1724, the building was roofed. It was soon afterward completed, and the entire cost of erection was ninety-four thousand dollars of our decimal currency. By his will he left, as an endowment for it, almost one million one hundred thousand dollars, making his whole gift for that institution almost twelve hundred thousand dollars. He also built an alms-house at Tamworth, in Staffordshire, for fourteen men and women; and he bequeathed to it a little over six hundred dollars a year. He also left an annuity of two thousand dollars to Christ's Hospital in London. Thomas Guy gave for charitable purposes more money than any private individual in the kingdom had ever done before; and he left to his few and remote relatives four hundred thousand dollars.

Our picture represents the entrance to Guy's Hospital from the quadrangle on its front, in the center of which

GUY'S HOSPITAL.

is a bronze statue of its Founder, by Scheemaker. The front panel of the pedestal bears the following inscription:

THOMAS GUY,

SOLE FOUNDER OF THIS HOSPITAL

IN HIS LIFETIME.

A. D. M DCC XXI.

On the west side of the pedestal is a representation, in low relief, of the scene of the Good Samaritan. On the south side is another, of Guy's arms; and on the east side is still another, representing our Saviour healing the impotent man.

From the time of his visit to the Hospital founded by his kinsman, Mr. Vassar dates his resolution to devote a large portion of his own fortune, "in his lifetime," to some benevolent purpose; and that of an asylum for the sick, to be established in the village in which he had accumulated his wealth, at once assumed a definite shape. He visited Guy's

Hospital frequently while he remained in London. He made himself familiar with its history, construction, equipment, and operations; and brought home with him much information, in the form of drawings and notes, for his guidance in his own plan of benevolence. And when he left his wife and Mr. Swan in London and traveled alone into Norfolk, to visit his birthplace, his thoughts were much occupied in the contemplation of the noble idea of becoming a benefactor of his race.

That visit to his birthplace was a most interesting circumstance in the life of Mr. Vassar. He traveled from London to Norwich by railway, and from that old city to East Dereham in a private carriage. The Homestead had often been a subject of his day-dreams when memory transported him back to childhood. The cottage, the pebbly pond, the gate, the stately trees, the meadows, the cultivated fields, and the gentle hills, were in those visions; and when he returned, after an absence of fifty years, they were all there! The pond seemed less, and the hills not so lofty, nor the cottage so high and long, as each appeared to his young eyes, and in the "pictures on memory's wall;" but a grand old hollow tree—hollow and dying when he left—was still there, and seeming as huge and grand as in his childhood. But it was now without leaf or acorn, and was clad only in the verdure of a luxuriant parasite. It seemed as if it might have been the study of Spenser when he wrote,—

> "A huge oak, dry and dead,
> Still clad with reliques of its trophies old,
> Lifting to heaven its aged, hoary head;
> Whose foot on earth hath got but feeble hold,
> And, half disboweled, stands above the ground
> With wreathèd roots and naked arms."

It was at the beginning of July, and scenes of the haymaking season, about which Herrick and others of the elder poets of England delighted to write, and which had been deeply impressed upon the pilgrim's young mind, were now reproduced and gave him great delight. "At that season," says Thomas Miller the Basket Maker, in one of his exquisite sketches of rural life in England, "silence reigns in the villages. If you knock at fifty doors you are likely to receive no answer, for old and young are in the fields; even the 'wee things' toddle along the smooth-shaven green, or roll happily among the windrows. First is the stout mower; he rises early in the morning, and long before the heat of the day comes on, he has leveled many a beautiful flower and healing herb to the earth. You hear him sharpening his scythe long before you can see him—the clear 'rasp, rasp,' rings far and wide over the valleys. Then you catch a glimpse of his white shirt-sleeves through some vista in the hedge, moving like the pendulum of a clock or the wings of a bird—you cannot distinguish clearly for the mists. At length you near him. What havoc has he made! what fair daughters of the field has he prostrated! what hidden homes has he laid bare!—haunts of the bird and field-mouse—unroofing the snug dwelling, and leaving their little ones exposed to the covetous glances of the nesting boys. . . . . Where will you find happier faces than in the hay-field? The farmer is there, moving like a father amongst his children, smiling occasionally at the innocent jest, or prophesying the wedding-day between Jane and John, who are following each other with the rake and fork. Then there is all the village gossip—what hours it takes telling! And there is the blushing damsel with her gown thrown off, and stripped to the stays, showing all the symmetry of her fine figure while raking round the haycock which her lover has reared, forgetful of the heat and labor in the enjoyment of his conversation. How proud he also seems who is mounted on the top of the wagon to arrange the load!—but still prouder he who forms the hay-stack in the farmyard! He will boast of its roundness, firmness, and regularity for many a night over his ale, and appeal to the old men, who, instead of answering him, will enter into a long narrative of the large stacks which they had formed when young men. . . . . There is a charm in scenes like these—a something that rushes upon the heart like the joyousness of boyhood—happiness felt, not seen."

London is less populous in July than in any other month, for its denizens have then fled from its heat to the cooler air of the mountains or the seashore. When Mr. Vassar returned from his little excursion, he and his companions followed the universal example, and departed for the coast of the Irish Sea. They passed by railway through the rich midland counties of England, to the immense manufacturing and commercial city of Manchester, on the Irwell, where they remained a few days, and then journeyed to Liverpool, on the Mersey, the chief sea-port of England. In each of these immense marts of business they spent time in observation most pleasantly and profitably. The great cotton manufactories of the former city, with their forty thousand operatives; and the magnificent docks of the latter, whose commercial marine is inferior only to that of New York, are among the wonders of the modern world.

When these, and scores of other objects of interest, had been seen in Liverpool, and in the ship-building borough of Birkenhead opposite, and there were no more novelties to excite our travelers, they crossed St. George's Channel in a steamer to Dublin—the Eblama of Ptolemy—the Bally-ath-Cliath of the ancient Celts and Milesians. There they remained several days, occupying every hour of daylight in seeing all that was attractive to the eye, and hearing all that was agreeable to the ear, in that fine city—looking upon its Castle on the hill; its institutions of learning; its public squares, with their columns and statues; its fine churches, with their paintings and decorations; its convents, asylums, hospitals, and zoological garden; its nine superb bridges that span the estuary on which the town is built, and the beautiful environs of that oldest city in Ireland. They extended one of their rides to Maynooth, on the Royal Canal, fifteen miles from Dublin, which is the seat of the College of St. Patrick, founded by act of Parliament for the education of Roman Catholics for the priesthood, and about which, concerning a repeal of the grant or the annual appropriations for its support, there were warm debates in the National Legislature for many years.

When Dublin was well studied, our travelers journeyed northward to Belfast, in the picturesque county of Antrim, where a little time was pleasantly spent; and then they crossed that interesting shire to the sea-coast, on the northern extremity of Ireland, to view the Giants' Causeway, that great basaltic wonder, that stretches along the borders of the ocean for eight miles, between the promontories of Bengore and Fairhead. They passed several days in that vicinity, and then crossing the North Channel in a steam-packet, voyaged up the Frith of Clyde to the City of Glasgow, whose foundations were laid seven centuries before. They went into its principal manufactories, ship-yards, and public buildings; its Green; its Kelvin Grove, which the pen of Burns immortalized; saw its monuments and statues; explored the University (with its thousand students and its forty thousand volumes) founded by Pope Nicholas the Fifth, four hundred years ago, and above whose turrets rises the lightning-rod placed there by Dr. Franklin, 1772; and they listened to the solemn pealing of the organ in the Cathedral of St. Mungo, whose foundation-stones were laid when good David the First was king of Scotland. Out in the suburbs and the surrounding country they wandered, and rested in their weariness upon the gray stones of the famous wall built by the Romans, from the Frith of Clyde to the Frith of Forth, when they were vainly attempting to subjugate the naked Caledonians. Then the travelers went down to Ayr—

> "Auld Ayr, wham ne'er a town surpasses
> In honest men and bonnie lasses;"

and strolled along the

> —"banks and braes o' bonnie Doon,"

not far distant, and around

> "By Alloway's auld haunted kirk,"

standing stark and roofless by the road-side between Ayr and Maybole, where Tam O' Shanter,

> "A blethering, blustering, drunken blellum,"

had the strange vision of

> "Warlocks and witches in a dance."

But most interesting of all was their visit to the birthplace of Burns, a long, low, and neat thatched cottage, with two windows and four doors in its front, situated on a pretty spot about two miles from Ayr. Near there, Burns's sister Isabella (Mrs. Beggs), who was one of a merry dancing-party on a July race-night, in 1782, was yet living, with her daughter. She was a kind-hearted, cheerful old lady, with whom our travelers spent several hours. They went to her house, as other strangers had done, without even a letter of introduction; but the genial sunshine of Mr. Vassar's nature was so sympathetic with her own that one would have supposed that they were old friends, they were so chatty. The party left the venerable sister of the poet laden with flowers and delighted with cheerful good-bys; and Mr. Vassar brought home with him, as a choice memento of his visit, a fac-simile of the manuscript of Burns's "Cotter's Saturday Night," presented to him by Mrs. Beggs.

After spending some time among the Lakes and Highlands of Scotland, Mr. Vassar and his little party made their way across the country to Stirling, where they visited the old castle in which the ancient Scotch kings dwelt and held high court. There they saw other remains of the Roman wall; and they visited the field of the famous battle of Bannockburn near by. Then they went down the Frith of Forth to Edinburgh, and in that city and its vicinity they tarried a week in visiting historical places, and literary and benevolent institutions.

Grandly picturesque is that old city of Edinburgh among the hills, and rich in incidents of Scottish history. Not one of its interesting localities escaped the eyes of our travelers, from the quaint dwelling of John Knox the Reformer, on High Street, or the trial-room of Jeanie Deans, to the lofty eminences that overlook the town. They climbed three hundred feet above the Forth to the Castle on a rock, and were rewarded by the sight of its vast armory; "Mons Meg," the huge Flemish cannon, wrought of bars and hoops of iron; and the regalia of the kings of Scotland—crown, scepter, sword, and wand. They climbed more than eight hundred feet above the Forth to Arthur's Seat, and were rewarded by the sight of one of the most charming and picturesque panoramas in the world. They visited Holyrood Palace, wherein the monarchs of Scotland held Court when it was a kingdom, and which was made famous by the deeds and misdeeds within its walls of the beautiful Queen Mary.

From Edinburgh Mr. Vassar and his companions traveled in a coach to Abbottsford on the Tweed, the very name of which awakens a sense of all that is romantic in Scottish history, tradition, and song; for it was there that Walter Scott, the "Wizard of the North," for a long time waved his pen-wand and summoned legions of characters, strange and familiar, noble and ignoble, ugly and beautiful, from all the past of his beloved Scotia, to charm the world of his own time and of all the future.

After visiting the abbeys of Dryburgh, Melrose, and Jedburgh, in the neighborhood of Abbottsford, the travelers crossed the Cheviot Hills on the border and were again in England. They journeyed leisurely to Newcastle-upon-Tyne, and after exploring the vast coal-mines in its vicinity, sometimes more than a thousand feet from the daylight, and visiting the finest Norman castle in all England, built there by Robert, son of William the Conqueror, they went to London, where they remained about three weeks. There they engaged an accomplished courier for a tour on the Continent, and crossed the southern borders of the North Sea to Antwerp, on the Scheldt, in Belgium, once the commercial center of Europe. Its citadel, built by the Duke of Alva three hundred years ago, summons to the student of history the terrible picture of that great siege, which the pen of Motley has described so picturesquely. Its immense fortifications, its superb cathedral, its great docks at which a thousand ships may be moored, its gallery of paintings, its botanical garden, and its manufactories, detained our travelers a few days. They made a short day's journey to Brussels, the beautiful capital of Belgium, so remarkable for the number and architecture of its ancient buildings, among which is the palace of the Prince of Orange. A ride of ten miles southward took them to the village of Waterloo, near which was fought the decisive battle which crushed the power and overthrew the young dynasty of Napoleon the First.

Returning to Brussels, Mr. Vassar and his companions traveled eastward to the old walled town of Cologne, on the Rhine, the capital of Rhenish Prussia, and remarkable as containing the finest cathedral in the world. From that city they went up that famous river, stopping at many places by the way. They were charmed, at first, by the sweet rural beauties along its borders, and the vineyards that clothed the gentle hills; and then by the grand and picturesque scenery among the mountains, from Bonn to Bingen, where castles in ruins and castles restored, as well as great vineyards, are most abundant. They spent a few days at the celebrated watering-places of Weisbaden and Baden-Baden; and a longer time at the free German city of Frankfort-on-the-Main, whose public squares, and promenades, and suburbs are not surpassed in beauty by any city in Europe.

From Frankfort our little party journeyed southward to Basle, on the upper Rhine, just within the borders of Switzerland; a picturesque and interesting town, founded in the fourth century, and famous, at one time, as the most powerful city in Helvetia. Around it cluster many historic associations, ancient and modern; and it is sanctified in the estimation of scholars by the tomb of Erasmus, who died there in 1536, and was buried in the old Roman Fort Basilia.

A short journey from Basle placed the travelers in Lucerne, on the Reuss, a highly picturesque town, inclosed by walls and watch-towers, and lying close by the beautiful cruciform lake of the same name. Upon the waters of that lake they made delightful excursions; and at Küssnacht, on its northern border, they sat in the chapel of William Tell, that stands near the spot where that glorious Swiss patriot, as tradition tells us, leaped from his boat and ended the career of Gessler, the oppressor of his country. Bryant has said:—

> "Chains may subdue the feeble spirit, but thee,
> Tell, of the iron heart, they could not tame!
> For thou wert of the mountains: they proclaim
> The everlasting Creed of Liberty."

When they departed from Lucerne they still kept a southward course, for it was Autumn, and the air was becoming cold among the mountains. They crossed the Lepontine Alps, at the St. Gothard Pass, nearly seven thousand feet above the Gulf of Venice, and descended into warm and beautiful Lombardy, to Milan, passing on the way the colossal statue of St. Borromeo, at Arona, on the borders of the beautiful Lake Maggiore. They had seen the spires of the magnificent cathedral while far away, rising from the center of the great city, which was famous as the chief town of Cisalpine Gaul centuries before the birth of Christ. The travelers spent several days among its wonders: the grand cathedral, with its four thousand four hundred statues; the immense hospital, founded by Sforza; Da Vinci's Last Supper, which he frescoed in the refectory of the old Dominican Convent;

the public library, with its one hundred and ninety thousand volumes; and a hundred other objects, ancient and modern, which there delight the eye and elevate the taste.

From Milan the party traveled by post to Genoa, a city so full of magnificence, bright and faded, that it is called "the superb." Its legendary history is older than the foundations of Rome; and its true story, running through long centuries, is almost as interesting as that of the capital of the Cæsars. Standing in the midst of its splendid architecture and its wealth of statuary; or looking up from its harbor, and seeing the city with its palaces and churches, and gardens and promenades rising like an amphitheater, with the bald summits of the Apennines and the icy peaks of the Alps towering grandly behind it, the beholder sympathizes with the Italian when he speaks of it as *la Superba.* Its attractive objects were diligently sought for by the travelers, and the most interesting of them all for intelligent Americans—the birthplace of Columbus—was visited with the greatest satisfaction.

After tarrying a few days in Genoa, the travelers went by steamer to Leghorn, the principal seaport of Tuscany, on the Mediterranean, which had long been famous for its manufactories of silk and straw. They journeyed into the interior to the walled town of Pisa, on the Arno. There they remained long enough to visit its attractions, such as the Campanile and the Leaning Tower; the Cemetery, with its huge mound of earth from Palestine; the Cathedral, built of pure marble, with magnificent doors of bronze and elegant columns from Greece; the richly adorned churches; the Ducal Palace and other public buildings; and its numerous works by the hands of painters and sculptors.

From Pisa they went up the Arno to Florence, at the foot of the Apennine mountains, which for generations has been the Mecca of the artist and scholar of all lands. It is peerless in its nativity record of really great men. There some of the brightest orbs in the galaxy of human genius arose upon the world. The poets Dante, Petrarch, Boccaccio, and Filicaja; the sculptor and painter Michael Angelo; the medalist, engraver, sculptor, musician, and soldier, Benvenuto Cellini; the statesmen and historians, Macchiavelli and Guicciardini; the astronomer Galileo; the painter Leonardo da Vinci; the discoverer of our own continent, Americus Vespucius; the great merchant, statesman, and benefactor, Cosmo de Medici, on whose tomb are the words applied to our beloved Washington: "Father of his Country"—and his greater grandson, Lorenzo the Magnificent, were all born there. The tombs of most of them the travelers saw in the Church of Sante Croce—the Valhalla or the Westminster Abbey of Tuscany; and their statues and monuments are everywhere in Florence. "You cannot stroll fifty yards," says D'Israeli—"you cannot enter a church or a palace, without being favorably reminded of the power of human thought. In Florence, the monuments are not only of great men, but of the greatest. You do not gaze upon the tomb of an author who is merely a great master of composition, but of one who formed the language. The illustrious astronomer is not the discoverer of a planet, but the revealer of the whole celestial machinery. The artists and the politicians are not merely the first sculptors and statesmen of their time, but the inventors of the very art and the very craft in which they excelled."

A simple catalogue of objects of interest in Florence

would fill many pages. The travelers looked upon all that were most remarkable, and then, returning to Leghorn, they went down the coast to Civita Vecchia, the chief sea-port of the Papal States. From that city they journeyed toward Rome, and on a beautiful afternoon they crossed the solitary Campagna, a great plain around it, strewn with the sad evidences of ancient splendor:—

"The Champaign, with its endless fleece
Of feathery grasses everywhere!
Silence and passion, joy and peace—
An everlasting wash of air—
Rome's ghost since her decease."

Rome! The greatest wonder in man's temporal history! No matter whether it is Truth or Fiction that tells you that a she-wolf gave sustenance to its founders. There it was, a thriving village, seven centuries before the Incarnation; there it was, the magnificient capital of the known world, at the Advent; there it is, a mighty ruin—a shriveled empire, just now fading out of sight as a sovereignty. It is yet filled with wonders; and what all travelers see in Rome our travelers saw, for they were diligent through every waking hour in exploring the present possessions of that once Mistress of the World, now seated among the nations in comparative squalor, with aspect sad and desolate. Her gorgeous decorations of modern churches and palaces seem unbecoming, for they make her real wretchedness appear more forbidding. And yet the curious and the learned sit with delight in her lap, admiring even her scars and wrinkles, because of the glorious associations which cluster around them; and they listen with enchanted ears to her marvelous stories of buried centuries with which her long and eventful life has been familiar. It was with reluctance that our travelers turned away from her, after lingering in her presence for weeks, for they had not yet felt the least satiety.

An incident illustrative of Mr. Vassar's indisposition for mere display occurred just before they left Rome. He purchased from different artists several statuettes, of various sizes, that gratified his taste. They were paid for and prepared for shipment, when he reflected that his modest home in Poughkeepsie was not an appropriate place for such works of art, and that they might be regarded by his fellow-townsmen as an ostentatious display of his wealth. There was no public place in the village in which they might have been appropriately

Mr. Vassar's Residence.

placed; so he left them in Italy, content to bring home some plain curiosities as mementoes of his visit to the crumbling Coliseum, or some other relic of the ancient city.

From Rome the travelers went to Naples—the Parthenope of the Greeks, who founded it. Sweetly it reposes in the most delicious climate, and on the borders of a bay that has no peer in extent and beauty. It has a stirring history since Virgil studied there and was buried in its suburbs; for the Emperors Adrian and Constantine made it their occasional residence; and Belisarius sacked it; and emperors of Germany and of Spain trod its streets as its masters by the fortunes of war; and earthquakes and its restless neighbor Vesuvius have rent and scarred it. How marvelous its neighborhood, where Pompeii and Herculaneum were for centuries hidden from the knowledge of man by the ashes that fell and the lava that flowed from lofty Vesuvius, before the wondering eyes of Pliny. That volcano was moderately active when our travelers were there, and climbed its black slopes. Before the writer is a piece of lava which Mr. Vassar drew from the fiery stream with a rude staff, and in it embedded an Italian copper coin.

When Naples and its near and remote environs had been explored, the travelers went to the Neapolitan island of Capri—delightful Capri—where Augustus sought health, and Tiberius, with his dozen villas and convivial friends, passed the evening of his days. They also went to Ischia, and enjoyed the luxury of the Sulphur Springs of Cassameccia, and the wines made from the delicious grapes of the island. Then they voyaged back to Genoa, and journeyed westward along the shores of the Mediterranean Sea, through Nice and Toulon to Marseilles, which Phœnician navigators founded almost as early as the beginning of Rome. There they remained a week, and then went northward to Lyons, on the Rhone, the second city in France in population and commercial importance. History has much to say about it. It was the capital of Celtic Gaul before the Christian era; kings of Burgundy dwelt there; and within its borders three Roman emperors were born. The fame of its silk manufactories is universal: and among its looms and other industrial implements of the great city our travelers spent a week.

From Lyons they went up to Geneva, in Switzerland, the "nursery of heresy," as Charles the Ninth called it, where Rousseau the free-thinker was born, and has been honored with a statue; and where Calvin thundered his anathemas alike against free-thinkers, the Papal hierarchy, and Servetus the Unitarian. They enjoyed the invigorating air and ennobling scenery in that delightful region, and wondered how, in such an atmosphere, Calvin could have consented to the slaughter of Servetus for "blasphemy and heresy," or founded the famous school of terrifying theologians. Calvin said, "Time is, for man, the antechamber of hell or heaven; mark it well." From Geneva, where he uttered the thought, a hundred thousand time-markers are sent out to the world every year in the form of exquisitely wrought watches, that men may obey the solemn injunction of the great Reformer.

Still northward our travelers journeyed when they left Geneva, and again crossing the border into France, they made their way to Chalons, famous as the place where the bulls of excommunication, hurled by the Popes against Henry the Fourth of France, were publicly burnt. Thence they traveled by *diligence* to Paris, which some sagacious Englishman has declared to be the American's ideal of heaven. There they remained about three weeks, seeing all that was most remarkable, and hearing all that was most delightful. Then they traveled by post to Havre, crossed the channel to Dover, and at near midwinter found themselves again in London. Although not a third of the period allotted for their absence had expired, arrangements were now made for a speedy return to America. Mrs. Vassar, who was very domestic in her tastes and habits, was yearning for the quiet and rest of her own home, for she was thoroughly weary of travel, and satiated by sight-seeing. So, after tarrying about three weeks in London, industriously seeking and obtaining knowledge of much that is profitable to be known, they went to Liverpool and embarked for New York, where they arrived late in February.

During his travels abroad, Mr. Vassar had talked much about the disposition of a large part of his fortune in a way that should best promote the general welfare of society, especially the community in which he had lived for more than half a century. He and his companions had frequent discussions as to the best method of accomplishing the desired result. An asylum for the afflicted; a school for the free academic education of the worthy poor; and an institution devoted exclusively to the education of girls, were objects which then and at different times afterward presented themselves for his consideration. The founding of a hospital after the plan of Guy's was a favorite desire of his heart, but circumstances caused another object not less important to engage his attention, and, for a time, to weaken his determination to establish in Poughkeepsie an asylum for the sick and infirm. A daughter of his sister Maria, Miss Lydia Booth, had for some years held a prominent place among the thorough educators of girls in the village, and her school was always filled with the children of the best known citizens. Her apartments became too limited for herself and pupils, and Mr. Vassar purchased for her use a dwelling on Garden Street, on the northern verge of the town. It was quite a spacious building, with ample grounds around it. It had once belonged to one of the Livingston family, and its roof had acquired a little local fame as the shelter of the exiled Bourbon of the Orleans line, Louis Philippe, afterward king of France, who was accompanied by Prince Talleyrand, the peerless diplomat, and political Vicar of Bray. It was situated upon an elevated knoll, overlooking much of the village and the surrounding country; and there Miss Booth established the *Cottage Hill Seminary*, which is now, with the same title, the more extensive Church school for young women, of which the Rev. George T. Rider is Rector and proprietor.

Mr. Vassar took a lively interest in his niece's seminary. He visited it frequently, and listened with satisfaction to Miss Booth's suggestions, that he might be a substantial benefactor by appropriating a part of his wealth for the founding of an institution for the education of her sex, which should be of a higher order than any then existing. The suggestion made a deep impression on his mind, and when, a few years afterward, it was again presented to him for consideration by another, supported by cogent reasons, his judgment readily yielded, and a most salutary result followed.

It was several years after Mr. Vassar's return from Europe before he decided upon the object of his intended benevolent action. Business again occupied much of his thoughts and time, and the revolving wheels of his daily life were soon running in their accustomed ruts of routine. Matters of public concern to the community of which he was a part, claimed his attention and active co-operation. He was called to the presidency of the Board of Trustees of the village; and at length, when it was determined by some of the citizens to establish a public cemetery near the town, Mr. Vassar was one of the most zealous promoters of the enterprise. He was chairman of a committee appointed at a public meeting to select suitable grounds for that purpose. Many places were examined, and the Committee finally reported in favor of a picturesque portion of a farm, of about fifty acres in extent, lying three-fourths of a mile south from the Court-House. Much of it was in a state of natural rudeness. Wooded knolls arose above tangled hollows. Springs gushed out from oozy little hill-sides, and formed rivulets that,

> "Wanton and wild, through many a green ravine
> Beneath the forest flowed."

A quaint old farm-house stood near a fine spring, and close by it was a Dutch barn. The aspect of these was consonant with the rude surroundings; and to utilitarians, who measure value by the scale of pecuniary profit, the domain was an unattractive, idle wild. But the Committee saw in that topographical rudeness the substantial elements out of which a most beautiful landscape might be fashioned by the hand of Taste—a place for the repose of mortality that might so charm the senses of the living that the aspect of the Angel of Death would not disturb the soul of the contemplative Christian within its borders, but lead him to feel, with Young, that

> "Death is the crown of life.
> Were death denied, poor man would live in vain.
> Death wounds to cure: we fall; we rise; we reign!
> Spring from our fetters; fasten in the skies;
> Where blooming Eden withers in our sight.
> Death gives us more than was in Eden lost.
> This King of Terrors is the Prince of Peace"

The Committee urged the citizens to purchase the grounds they had selected. But there was hesitation. There was delay in the organization of a Cemetery Association. Other parties were bargaining for the ground. It might be sold, and the only spot that then seemed to be a suitable one for a cemetery would be lost to the citizens. To secure it for that purpose, Mr. Vassar, acting upon the impulses of his own judgment, and at the solicitation of his associates (James Bowne and Egbert B. Killey), purchased the property for the sum of eight thousand dollars. He held it for several months, waiting for the citizens to decide whether it should be used for a cemetery. He offered to sell it for that purpose at the price he had paid for it, and to take shares in the stock of the proposed association to the amount of one thousand dollars.

Springside in 1851.

In the mean time, Mr. Vassar had commenced improvements of the property in a manner suitable for a cemetery or the pleasure-grounds of a private residence. Because of the numerous fountains that were bubbling up here and there, he named the place Springside. The late A. J.

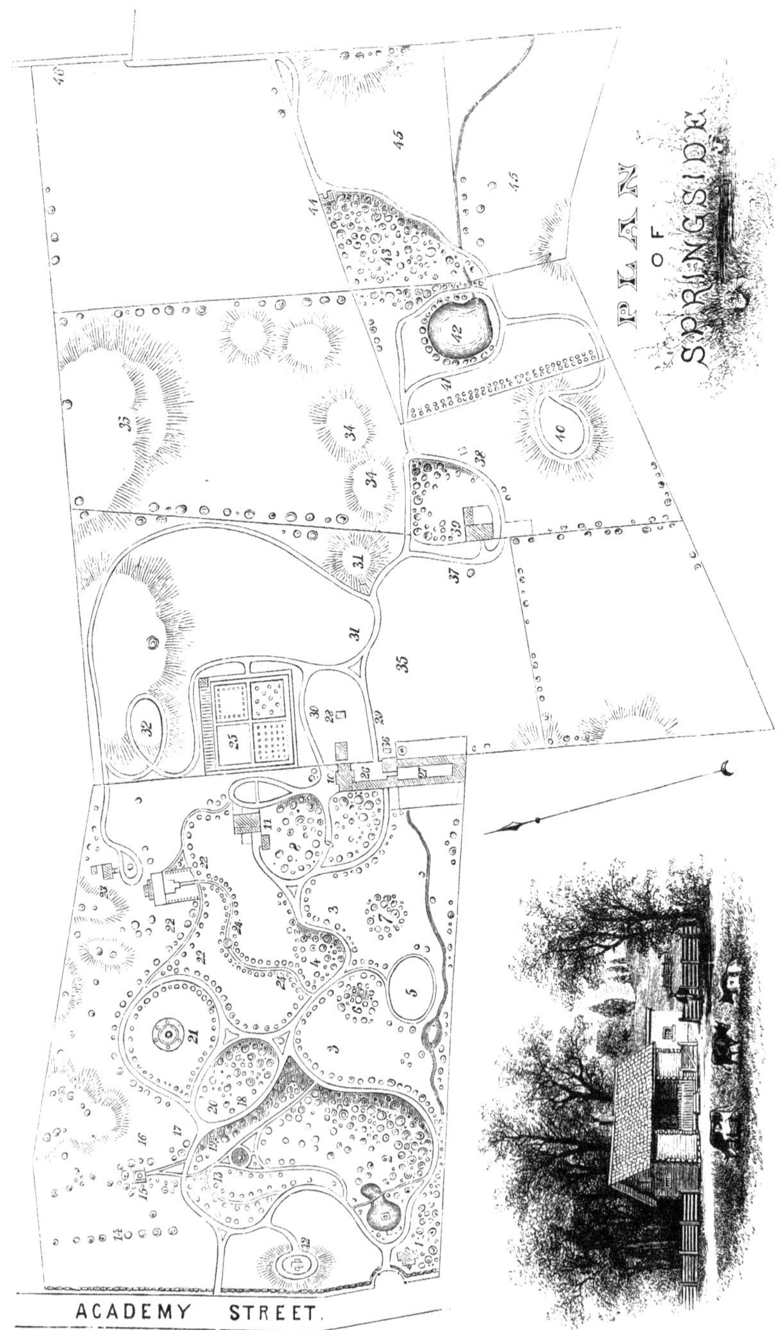
PLAN
OF
SPRINGSIDE
ACADEMY STREET.

Downing, the eminent rural architect and landscape-gardener, was called to explore it, suggest a plan of avenues for walks and drives, and a design for a portal and porter's lodge. William C. Jones, an Engineer of the Hudson River Railroad Company, made a correct topographical map of it for Mr. Vassar. Laborers were employed in the ruder task of preparing the grounds for the more skillful workmen who, in time, wrought out that beautiful creation of Nature and Art, the Springside of to-day.

The Cemetery Association was formed, but other grounds, not far distant, lying on the bank of the Hudson River, were purchased for its use, and Mr. Vassar determined to make Springside a place of delight for himself, his friends, and his fellow-citizens. From the designs of Mr. Downing, a porter's lodge, a cottage, barn, carriage-house, ice-house and dairy-room, granary, an aviary for wild and domestic fowls, an apiary, a spacious conservatory and neat gardener's cottage, and a log cabin on the more prosaic portions of the domain, where meadows and fields of grain may be seen, were erected. The primitive forest-trees on the knolls were left to grow on, untouched; the hollows and ravines were transformed into beautiful narrow paths or broad road-ways; a deer-park was laid out and peopled with tenants from the woods; *jets d'eau* and little hollows filled with sparkling waters were formed; and in the course of years more than one hundred thousand dollars were added to the first cost of the then almost profitless acres. Visitors agree that those acres, beautified and cultivated, are not surpassed by any spot in our country, of equal area, in variety of surface, pleasant views and vistas, near and remote, and picturesque effects everywhere.

Let us go in and look at the pictures from every point of vision. Suppose it to be a bright day in blossoming May, or leafy June, or when the ripening warmth of the months of the Lion or the Virgin prevails, or one of the delicious Ember-days, before the herald hoar-frosts have announced the near approach of Winter. Suppose it to be at the "Artists' hour" of the day, when every object casts a long shadow in the level rays of the declining sun, and the forms and lines of nature appear most distinct and beautiful. And let us take with us the topographical map on page 62, whose reference figures are indices to the names and places of objects to be seen within the domain.

We are now on a public avenue leading south from the city, and on the summit of the hill that overlooks the outward portions of Springside. On our right, nestled at the foot of the sunny slope of that hill, is "Woodside," the residence of G. C. Burnap, with its fine stone mansion, and fruitful vineyard, and elegant lawn of richest and softest verdure; and a little beyond are the meadows and groves of a portion of Linlithgow, the estate of the late Colonel Henry A. Livingston. On our left and opposite is a grassy bank supported by a cut-stone wall, fringed along its top with a trimmed hedge of Arbor Vitæ (*Thuja occidentalis*), or Flat Cedar shrubs. These mark the line of Springside along the public highway. Twenty miles before us we see the blue lines of the Hudson Highlands and the Fish Kil Mountains, with a rich farming country in the fore and middle grounds; and a little to the right we have glimpses of the river, and the picturesque country on its western borders. Nearer rise the rugged crags of Mine Point, covered with the dark spruce, the lighter cedar, and deciduous trees of great variety, at the foot of which Robert Juet, the journalist of some of Hudson's voyages, says the navigator landed, and communed by signs with the awed Indians. And nearer still are seen the grounds, in sweet repose, and the monuments and shrubbery, of the Rural Cemetery

ENTRANCE TO SPRINGSIDE.

We are now at the foot of the hill, and here is the south entrance to Springside (1), with the Porter's Lodge on the right. How pleasant is this broad, gravelly road, leading to the right into the most welcome shades! Let us turn from it for a few minutes and follow this little path to the left, up to the head of the gourd-shaped lake-

9

let near the Lodge, in the middle of which you see, embowered in evergreens, the breeding-house of the water-fowl that inhabit it. This is a cool retreat at the foot of Maple Hill (2), from which we may observe the visitors that ride or stroll in at this hour, from the highway. What a delicious breeze!

> "All the green herbs
> Are stirring in its breath; a thousand flowers,
> By the roadsides and borders of the brook,
> Nod gayly to each other; glossy leaves
> Are twinkling in the sun, as if the dew
> Were on them yet; and silver waters break
> Into small waves, and sparkle as it comes."

Let us go out again into the broad South Avenue. If we keep continually to the right, we shall pass every spot and object of interest, and return without difficulty to our place of departure. On our right, as we leave the foot of Maple Hill, a conical knoll, covered mostly with sugar-trees intermingled with the chestnut, beech, and a few oaks, is the Deer-park (3), through which runs a clear brook fringed with long grass and wild flowers. It is, as you see, partly a little savanna, with a solitary Norway spruce tree in its center. If we follow this brook, we shall soon reach Rock Roost (6), a rough mass of slate-rock twenty or thirty feet in height, with a dip of forty-five degrees, covered chiefly with oaks, and crowned by a single cedar tree. This path that leads around its base diverges here to the right and crosses the brook, over a rustic bridge at the head of a pebbly duck-pond, to an equally rustic cabin roofed with pantiles. This forms a covering for the deer, in inclement weather, which are kept in the wire-girt close adjoining. The cabin is overshadowed by a large tree, and forms a picturesque feature in the landscape.

We will return to Rock Roost, cross the savanna, made pleasant by the sweet odor of the mown grass, and re-enter South Avenue at its junction with Locust Grove Drive and North Avenue. Here is a beautiful little pond, reflecting the deep blue of the sky above, and glowing with gold fishes. Look up to the left among the trunks and branches of tall trees and the more modest evergreen shrubs, and see, on the summit of this high knoll, how weird appear those huge upright stones, standing here like palisades, and there like solitary sentinels guarding some mysterious spot. This is called Stonehenge (4), because of its suggestiveness of those strange remains of the Druids found at a place of that name in England. These hints serve to make us speculate a little on that ancient priesthood that came from the far East, and held supreme sway over the minds of millions of the Pagan world. Who knows, friend, whether they were not of the Zoroastrian Magi — the "Wise men of the East" — who went wondering and adoring to the Manger in Bethlehem in which lay the infant Redeemer? These Druids discoursed of the hidden nature of things; of the extent of the Universe; of the forms and motions of the stars; of the virtues of plants, and of the essence, power, and mode of action of the gods. Under huge oaks they built their colossal altars, and—but come, friend, if we linger here the sun will leave us in darkness as profound as that of the theology of the Druids; so let us pass on from this tiny "Stonehenge" and see what is here on the right of the Avenue. It is a gentler knoll, covered with the forest trees; and between it and Rock Roost is a wild, shaded hollow (5), called Group Gap. A path through it will lead us back to the brook, so we will pass on along the Avenue to the Cottage, a part of which appears above the tops of the little trees that surround it.

THE COTTAGE.

But what is this on our right? It is a charming grassy hollow, only a little below the level of the Avenue, open to the sun, and surrounding another shady knoll, thickly covered with deciduous and evergreen trees, with groups of loose stones, over which vines creep and blossom. This open girt of meadow (7) is called Little Belt.

Here is a gate at the entrance to a shaded lane that leads up to the rear of the Cottage in which Mr. Vassar has resided several summers. How thick the evergreens are, and how odorous their out-breathings!

On each stone gate-post sits a greyhound of iron, harmless in aspect and nature; but a little way up the path is a black-and-tan sentinel, giving most vehement warnings to the inmates of the castle of the approach of strangers. Let him bark to his heart's content. We have no desire to go up that private way; so we will pass along Cottage Avenue (9) to the grounds in front. Listen a moment to the pleasant voices on the left. They come from the summit of this shaded little hill, covered with large trees, hemlock saplings, and groups of stones, among which are rustic seats. This is Knitting Knoll (8), close by the Cottage, whereon it is pleasant to sit and chat

Cottage Avenue Gate.

at this delightful hour, while the busy fingers make the worsted meshes grow into beauteous forms and tints.

The Cottage Avenue gate is like the heart of the owner—wide open with welcome to all friends. The surmountings of its stone posts appear a little more formidable than those of the other gate. On one is a wild boar couchant, reminding us of fierceness; on the other a fox in similar attitude—the accepted token of cunning. These are the antitheses of the character of the Master of Springside.

We will not visit the cottage yet, for we have a long way to travel before we may rest; so let us turn a little back and follow the main Avenue to that archway yonder, that connects a range of edifices on opposite sides of the road. Here we are in the midst of buildings of pleasing patterns. On one hand are the coach-house (10), the farm stables and office (26), the ice-house and dairy-rooms, and fancy bird-houses (28) with glass fronts; and on the other side are the granary (36) and the aviary for wild fowls (27), covered with an open ceiling of wire to prevent the escape of the birds. Here, at one time, might have been found a most interesting chapter in the history of animated nature. Here flashed a golden pheasant in the sun; there a white heron performed amusing gambols; yonder, beautiful gazelles were skipping; wood-ducks were sporting in tiny lakes; a great variety of hares and rabbits were burrowing; peacocks were strutting in the pride of their iridescent plumage; a white cockatoo was talking egotistically of itself as "Pretty Poll;" a sociable Mexican pheasant, with eyes charmed by glittering things, followed you everywhere; and the whole air was vocal with the love-songs of a hundred doves of the rarest kind. These have given place to those sober house-keepers, the domestic fowl, but of the most aristocratic families, from the plump Bantam of Java to the tall gawky of Shanghai.

Leaving this group of buildings, we enter Dale Avenue (29), with Meadow Girt (35) on our right, which is irrigated by the same brook that flows through the Deer-park. Across it are lying the long shadows of trees that deepen the tints of green covering its bosom. On the left, at the parting of the ways, that tall larch stands like a sentinel, its grace forming a positive contrast to the covering of that high rocky hill, with its uncouth commingling of elm and maple, hickory and birch, chestnut and ash trees, and tangled shrubs, and interlacing vines and brambles—a rude spot, which the owner has appropriately called Scraggy Knoll (31). Along the base of this wild hill, and all around to the plain farm-barn and out-buildings on the eastern verge of Meadow Girt, is Chestnut Drive (37), a roadway lined on the right with a row of the most vigorous of those oriental trees known as the *hippocastanum*, or horse-chestnut.

At the barn we will pass through a gate, and take the winding road up to the summit of the lofty eminence on our right, to Hill Girt (40). Now look around you: all of Springside is at your feet, and the view opens broadly in every direction. A few residences in the suburbs of the city are seen here; there you have glimpses of the Hudson, and the white sails upon its bosom; and yonder (how purple they are!) rise the Fish Kil and Canterbury Mountains, on whose summits the beacon-fires of patriots blazed in the time of the old War for Independence.

The sun is much nearer the horizon than when we started, and we must pass on: let us go down near the barn, and out into Dale Avenue, by these clumps of cedars and chestnuts on the left of South Pass Drive (38), and that magnificent hemlock that stands on the steep slope of a knoll. Here, to the right, is the Semicircular Road (41), passing along the margin of a fine orchard of that delicious fruit from Corinth which is seen in almost every garden in the temperate zone. Here grow some of the finest red and white currant-shrubs, and when they are in blossom, or covered with clustering fruit, they form a pleasing neighborhood to the sparkling Perch Pond (42) near by, which we pass as we go around to the gate that opens into Glen Vale (45). See what a pretty hollow among gentle hills this is! It is watered by the same brook that we have met several times in our ramble. Yonder, to the right, is an open oak grove, shading the smooth-shaven sward on the slope. Here, on the left, is a wild region called Woody Glen (43), in which art has refrained from interfering with nature. Every thing is left as the owner found it. Among the trees that shoot up from a thick undergrowth of shrubs, witch-hazel, and low creeping vines, in which wild rabbits find homes, squirrels abound; and there the drum of the partridge and the quail's call for "Bob White" may be heard. It forms a rude contrast to Glen Vale, and a picturesque background for Uncle Tom's Cabin (44), pictured on the map of Springside that you carry in your hand. It is a comfortable log house, covered with tiles, in which live the family of the teamster of the domain. It stands at the edge of the wood; and near it a private farm-road (46) passes through Mr Vassar's outer grounds to the public highway, south-eastward of the city.

Here we will turn back and retrace our steps as far as Scraggy Knoll. As we leave Woody Glen and the Perch Pond, the gentle eminences on our right are the Eden Hills (34), without trees or shrubs, and enlivened by a herd of fine Devonshire cattle. These hills offer a pleasant ramble on a cool day in Autumn, when the groves and forests are clothed in the gorgeous drapery of mid-October. Prospect Hill (33), of this range, rises high above the others, and affords an extensive view of the surrounding country. We have not time to go up there now; so we will pass along to the foot of Scraggy Knoll, and take this road to the right; it will lead us, in the shade of maple trees, along the margin of an orchard up to Poplar Summit Drive (32), on an eminence of about

VIEW FROM POPLAR SUMMIT DRIVE.

the same altitude as Prospect Hill. Do you see those tall and slender Lombardy poplars, shooting up on our left among the pines and flat cedars just above the orchard, and with them forming a beautiful thicket on the slope? These suggested the name for this drive. A little below us we see the heavy wall of the Flower and Kitchen Garden (25), that backs the cold grapery there; and a little lower

10

still is the group of buildings connected with the archway already mentioned. How pleasing is this view also, overlooking as it does much of Springside, and some fine estates south of it, and terminating in the range of mountains twenty miles distant, of which Beacon Hill is the most lofty.

We will pass down by this evergreen hedgerow, and then between the orchard and the Flower and Kitchen Garden to Lack Lawn Knoll (30), near the Carriage-house. It is a pretty spot, covered with grass and shaded by larches and pines. The curious little building on the right, at the corner of the garden, is the Apiary, whose vane, an enormous golden honey-bee swinging over a hive, denotes its use. We will pass around this to the cottage. How pleasant is this carriage-way, of oval form, in front of the house. It is hemmed in by lofty ever-green trees, and its margin is ornamented with a series of comic statuettes, exquisitely wrought from light gray stone, to illustrate phases of character in social life in Italy, where they were made. At the pretty Cottage (11) we are sure of a cordial welcome.

Not at home? Although it is near the close of this long afternoon, the Founder of Vassar College, who has been rewarded for his fidelity in his stewardship of wealth by length of days and the full consummation of his designs and wishes, has not yet returned from his accustomed visit to the stately memorial of his beneficence, in the work of which his heart is so warmly sympathetic. So we will pass on to the Grapery and Greenhouse grounds (22), and the Gardener's cottage (23), either by Cottage Avenue around Stonehenge, or by this beautiful winding path to the right, so closely fringed on one side with a dark hemlock hedge, and on the other by pine, larch, and cedar trees.

We will follow the path. How pleasantly the grounds open before us on that gentle slope on which the Con-

THE CONSERVATORY AND GARDENER'S COTTAGE.

servatory stands with its crystal roofs, covering in Winter clusters of luscious grapes, many rare exotics, and domestic flowering shrubs and plants in great abundance. Now, these are all out upon the grounds around, beautifying a hundred places, and loading this evening air with fragrance. Delicately Barry Cornwall says—

> "Like sweet thoughts that come
> Winged from the maiden fancy, and fly off
> In music to the skies, and there are lost,
> These ever-steaming odors seek the sun,
> And fade in the light he scatters."

Here is a narrow lane with a wall of neatly trimmed

cedar shrubs on each side, higher than our heads. Let us see where and to what surprise it will lead us. Have the almond-eyed Celestials been here? Have the degenerate disciples of Confucius been planting a little seed of paganism in Springside? This little Pagoda (24) makes us think of the far Orient, where, in secluded places like this, little temples are sacred shrines. But where is the idol? Ask the lovers who have strolled through these beautiful grounds and rested beneath this little roof. They have seen and worshiped it here in human form and substance, though it may be invisible to us.

THE PAGODA.

Still farther on this secluded pathway leads us. It winds gently upward, and leaves us among the rude rocks of Stonehenge. Here, on this immense bench of graywacke, we may rest a few minutes, for the sun yet lingers above the horizon, and our pleasant ramble is nearly ended. Sounds of mirth come up from the Deer-park below, where a bevy of girls are gathering wild flowers. Did Francis Sachetti have a scene like this for his inspirations when he said in rhyme—

'Walking and musing in a wood, I saw
Some ladies gathering flowers—now this, now t'other,—
And crying in delight to one another,
'Look here, look here! what's this? a fleur-de-lis,
Oh! get some violets there;—
No, no,—some roses farther onward there;
How beautiful they are!
Oh me! those thorns do prick so—only see!—
Not that—the other—reach it me.

Hallo, Hallo! what is it leaping so?
A grasshopper! a grasshopper!'"

This rude wood-path leads us down to the little pond already mentioned, where the gold fishes live, and we find a beautiful open hollow before us, called Center Circle (21), around which passes a fine avenue. From this road the eye is continually charmed by pleasant surprises. The Circle is hemmed in by rows and groups of evergreen and deciduous trees, and above these tower loftily a large oak and two huge black-walnut trees. Yonder is seen a heap of stones almost hidden by running roses; and all about us are sweet flowering shrubs. In the center is a jet of water, falling into two basins and a pool, one above the other, in sparkling cascades. Around these are vases filled with flowers; and between them and the road is a lawn covered with soft grass.

On completing the Circle, we come to the Villa Site (16), and Lawn Terrace (17), on the right. Let us climb this bank of greensward. How pretty is this semicircular lawn, ten feet above the carriage-way, and fringed with young pine and spruce trees. Twenty or thirty feet higher is the Villa Site, on which Mr. Vassar contemplated building a residence for himself and family. It is dotted with ancient apple-trees, and commands some pleasant distant views of the river, and the country on its borders, and of Springside near. From this hill we may go down a steep, rough bank, through a grove of locusts, to Walnut Row (14), where another beautiful lawn lies basking in the evening sun, on the outer border of the domain.

Turn now a little to the left, by these ancient cherry-trees, and see how grandly this giant sycamore—one of the primitive sons of the forest—rises above the surrounding trees, and spreads its sheltering branches over the spring at its foot. In this overshadowing it is assisted by an ancient willow, on the other side of the spring that bubbles up in copious measure beneath that arch of masonry, on the top of which reposes the iron image of a watch-dog. Delicious is the draught of water from its cool reservoir; and we turn away refreshed as we follow Willow Spring Walk (15) out to Locust Grove Drive (18), that comes up between the Ever-green Parks (19–20).

WILLOW SPRING.

This walk is shaded by the *Salix Babylonica*, or Weeping Willow, and leads out by a flower-vase to the head of Jet Vale Path (13), by which we will go down to one of the most secluded and beautiful places in Springside. Here, between the Ever-green Parks and Maple Hill, the water that flows down from Willow Spring leaps up from the mouth of an image of a fluttering swan, and, falling in drops and spray, forms a sparkling pool around it. How truly charming is this cool place at the evening hour! Every thing around us is in shadow, and the exhalations of

Jet Vale Fountain.

flowers burden the air with fragrance. Through the interlacing branches where the golden sunlight is playing, we have glimpses of the Summer-house (12) on the little hill by the highway around which Summit Avenue passes, and this is all we may see of the world without, excepting the sky above us and the illuminated tops of distant trees. There is here a repose and an aspect that may remind us of the poet's description of the place

> "Where our primeval Parents found sweet rest."

Milton says—

> "* * * * * It was a place
> Chosen by the Sovereign Planter, when He framed
> All things to man's delightful use: the roof
> Of thickest covert was inwoven shade,
> Laurel and myrtle, and what higher grew
> Of firm and fragrant leaf; on either side
> Acanthus, and each odorous bushy shrub
> Fenced up the verdant wall; each beauteous flower,
> Iris all hues, roses, and jessamine,
> Reared high with flourished heads between, and wrought
> Mosaic; under foot the violet,
> Crocus, and hyacinth, with rich inlay
> Broidered the ground, more colored than with stone
> Of costliest emblem."

This little path to the left will lead us down to the Porter's Lodge, and this one up to the Summer-house, where we may watch the sun as it goes down behind the western hills. Is it a familiar sight? Very well; then we will walk along this winding path to South Avenue and the portal, and go out into the highway homeward bound, with the treasures of the delightful experience of a summer evening ramble in SPRINGSIDE.

During the years while cares of business, and public duties, and the delights of Springside, as it developed into greater perfection, were occupying much of Mr. Vassar's thoughts and time, he had not been unmindful of his generous resolutions concerning the disposition of a large portion of his fortune. His project of benevolent action, though not yet possessing definite shape, remained a fixed purpose, and was the subject of frequent conversation with his most intimate friends, for he had determined to execute it during his lifetime. At length his niece, who had planted and fostered in his mind the idea of founding a model School for young women, died suddenly. Cottage Hill Seminary was closed; and for a while the subject of the education of woman was less in Mr. Vassar's thoughts as a practical matter than the founding of a hospital. The latter object commanded his most serious attention, and he had taken important steps preliminary to the establishment, in Poughkeepsie, of an extensive asylum for the comfort and cure of the sick, when circumstances turned the tide of his thoughts and desires again in a strong current toward the great work proposed by his niece.

In the Spring of 1855, Cottage Hill Seminary was purchased and reopened by Professor M. P. Jewett, who had been for several years at the head of a large school for young women in Alabama, known as the "Judson Female Institute." He united himself in fellowship with the congregation of the Central Baptist Church, of which Mr. Vassar was an active member, and between them the most friendly and confidential relations were soon formed. When the topic that occupied so much of Mr. Vassar's thoughts became a subject of conversation between them, Dr. Jewett suggested that he might become a greater benefactor to his race by erecting and endowing a college for young women—an institution that should be to their sex what Yale and Harvard are to our own—than by any other act. Here was the noble idea of Miss Booth amplified. The project at once commended itself to Mr.

11

Vassar's judgment, and awakened a desire to carry it out on a scale commensurate with his generous impulses.

Millions of dollars had been spent in founding and building up the numerous colleges for young men in the United States, while not a single college for young women had been established. The need of such institutions was felt by many of the best educators in the country, and had begun to occupy the serious attention of statesmen and philanthropists. The importance of the thorough education of women in every department of learning is a manifest necessity in our land, whose free institutions rest, or should rest, on the solid foundations of the virtue and intelligence of the people. Lord Brougham made the wise and indisputable assertion, that "the character and destiny of human beings are generally fixed before the child is ten years of age." That character and destiny are almost always molded, in the largest degree, by the mother, for she is the "prophet, priest, and king" of the household to the trusting little child, and commands its faith, reverence, and obedience. Pressing, then, is the need of her thorough preparation for the triple duty, by the acquirement of that power which comes from the most comprehensive knowledge of "things temporal and things spiritual."

Already, in response to the mute but potential appeals of that need, the "American Woman's Educational Association" had been formed in the City of New York, whose avowed object was to secure to American women a liberal education, by the establishment of permanent endowed institutions for the young of their sex that should embrace the leading features of colleges for young men. Already schools had been put in successful operation by that society. The Baptists of Massachusetts had also practically acknowledged the need, by establishing the "Ladies' Collegiate Institute," at Worcester, in that State, with an endowment of two hundred thousand dollars: and other denominations were considering not only the propriety, but the necessity, of founding and endowing similar institutions.

Mr. Vassar clearly perceived that the time was auspicious for him to act. He was offered the opportunity of leading in a cause of enlightened benevolence of the most profound interest to his country and mankind, in which numbers might follow, but none might go before. To him were proffered the high privilege and the peculiar honor of actually establishing and putting into operation the *first* grand, permanent, endowed college for Young Women ever projected, and he gladly accepted the boon, with a sincere desire to become a real public benefactor. While considerations of personal honor to be gained by the act could not alone have excited his ambition with a craving appetite for such aliment, he would have been less or more than human if the expectation of such honor had not been a stimulant to action; for, as Young says—

"The love of praise, howe'er concealed by art,
Reigns more or less in every human heart.
The proud, to gain it, toils on toils endure;
The modest shun it but to make it sure."

And Spenser, the polished limner of human nature, significantly inquires—

"Who would ever care to do brave deed,
Or strive in virtue others to excel,
If none should yield him his deservèd meed,
Due praise, that is the spur of doing well?
For if good were not praisèd more than ill,
None would choose goodness of his own free will."

Mr. Vassar was always an eminently practical man, and his wisdom and prudence were never more conspicuous than in his slow and cautious approach to a conclusion upon a subject of such vast importance as that which now occupied his most anxious thoughts. Satisfied of that importance in a moral, social, and political point of view, he brought the whole matter to the test of practical business calculations; for every human enterprise needs human sustenance, and upon that sustenance, formed after the fashion of the laws of trade, its life depends. A correspondence, oral and epistolary, was opened with some of the leading educators of the land, and among them Professor Jewett was one of his most frequent and confidential advisers. To the eminent school architect, the late Thomas A. Tefft, then residing in Providence, Rhode Island, Dr. Jewett submitted in writing a general description of a building or buildings that might accommodate four hundred pupils, with a full complement of Professors and Tutors; and from him he procured designs, and estimates of cost. These were submitted to Mr. Vassar's rigid scrutiny, and the result was a determination on his part to erect and endow, during his lifetime, a college for Young Women, on a magnificent scale, in the most perfect manner, and upon the most liberal basis, in which neither sect nor creed should have a controlling influence, as such. He was warmly attached to the Baptists by life-long associations, and a greater number of educated men and educators whom he consulted about his projected enterprise were of that denomination; but when it was proposed to have the college placed under the general control of Baptists, Mr. Vassar's more catholic spirit instantly and emphatically dissented.

And in his address to the Trustees of the College, at the organization of the Board, five years later, he expressed his wishes on that point decidedly, in the following brief sentence, which is here given in a fac-simile of his handwriting when he was seventy-five years of age.

All sectarian influences should be carefully excluded; but the training of our Students should never be intrusted to the skeptical, the irreligious or immoral.

Time passed on. Mr. Vassar wished to have his two nephews (Matthew and John Guy Vassar, who were yet his business partners, and each, like himself, childless and the possessor of a large fortune) associated with him in the enterprise, that they might share with him the delightful task and the deserved honors incident to the execution of his beneficent design; for, if it should be successful, it would be an everlasting memorial of the Vassar name. That earnest desire of his heart was not gratified; and he proceeded to plant the seed, and reap the bountiful harvest of blessings which springs from well-doing, without their co-operation.

This conclusion was reached in the Spring of 1860, and Mr. Vassar, then nearly seventy years of age, determined to carry out his long-cherished plan at once. Dr. Jewett was chosen to be his chief co-worker in the great labor. That he might devote his whole time to the task, he sold the Cottage Hill Seminary property, and relinquished the school at the close of the Summer term. An extensive correspondence on the subject of the college, personal and by writing, was kept up during the Autumn, and preparations were made for procuring a charter for the projected College from the Legislature of the State of New York. The charters of a large number of institutions of learning in the United States, for both sexes, were carefully examined; and these labors resulted in the draft of a bill by Mr. Swan, who, during all the years of inquiry and discussion of the subject of Mr. Vassar's beneficent projects, had been one of his most friendly counselors. It was a model of brevity and comprehensiveness. In it the name of "Vassar Female College" was given to the projected institution. That name was changed by an act of the Legislature on the first day of February, 1867, at the request of the

VASSAR COLLEGE SEAL.

Board of Trustees, by the omission of the word "Female." The corporate title is now VASSAR COLLEGE.

When the Bill was introduced in the Legislature, and the greatness of Mr. Vassar's plans was made apparent, the liveliest interest. amounting to enthusiasm, was manifested.

Leading members of both Houses paid eloquent tributes of praise to the projector, and warmly eulogized this exhibition of a noble spirit and almost princely munificence. The reporters of the principal daily newspapers of the State sent abroad from the Capitol the most glowing details of the novel and magnificent enterprise; and the attention of the whole country was soon directed to Poughkeepsie and the Founder of Vassar College. The act for its incorporation passed on the 18th of January, 1861, having been pressed through both Houses in advance of all other bills. It was the first or second bill of that session of the Legislature that received the signature of the Governor, Edwin D. Morgan, and became a law.

The following is a copy of the Charter:—

AN ACT
TO INCORPORATE VASSAR FEMALE COLLEGE.

Passed January 18th, 1861.

The People of the State of New York, represented in Senate and Assembly, do enact as follows:

SECTION 1. Matthew Vassar, Ira Harris, William Kelly, James Harper, Martin B. Anderson, John Thompson, Edward Lathrop, Charles W. Swift, E. L. Magoon, S. M. Buckingham, Milo P. Jewett, Nathan Bishop, Matthew Vassar, Jr., Benson J. Lossing, E. G. Robinson, Samuel F. B. Morse, S. S. Constant, John Guy Vassar, William Hague, Rufus Babcock, Cornelius Dubois, John H. Raymond, Morgan L. Smith, Cyrus Swan, George W. Sterling, George T. Pierce, Smith Sheldon, Joseph C. Doughty, and A. L. Allen, are hereby constituted a body corporate, by the name of "Vassar Female College," to be located in Duchess county, near the city of Poughkeepsie. By that name the said corporation shall have perpetual succession, with power to fill vacancies as they may occur from time to time in their board, to sue and be sued, to contract and be contracted with, to make and use a common seal and to alter the same at pleasure, to purchase, take, and hold, by gift, grant, or devise, subject to "an Act relating to wills," passed April 13th, 1860, except in the case of Matthew Vassar, herein named, and to dispose of, any real and personal property, the yearly income or revenue of which shall not exceed the value of forty thousand dollars.

§ 2. The object and purpose of said corporation are hereby declared to be, to promote the education of young women in literature, science, and the arts.

§ 3. The college may grant to students under its charge diplomas or honorary testimonials, in such form as it may designate. It may also grant and confer such honors, degrees, and diplomas as are granted by any university, college, or seminary of learning in the United States.

§ 4. Diplomas granted by the college shall entitle the possessors to the immunities and privileges allowed by usage or statute to the possessors of like diplomas from any university, college, or seminary of learning in this State.

§ 5. The persons named in the first section of this act shall be the first trustees of the said corporation. The president of the college, while holding office, shall be a member of the board of trustees.

§ 6. Nine trustees shall be a quorum for the transaction of business; but no real estate shall be bought or sold, and no president or professor of the college shall be appointed or removed, except by the affirmative vote of a majority of all the trustees.

§ 7. The corporation shall have all such powers, and be subject to such duties and liabilities as are applicable to colleges, and are specified or contained in the second and fifth articles of the first title of the fifteenth chapter of the first part of the revised statutes, and in title third, chapter eighteen of the same part of the revised statutes, except so far as the same are inconsistent with the provisions of this act.

§ 8. Matthew Vassar, of Poughkeepsie, is hereby authorized and empowered to give, grant, devise, and bequeath to the aforesaid corporation, by his last will and testament, or otherwise, any such portion of his estate as he may choose so to give, grant, devise, or bequeath, any existing act or statute to the contrary notwithstanding.

§ 9. This act shall take effect immediately.

The twenty-eight persons chosen by Mr. Vassar to constitute the "body corporate" of the College, and to be its first Trustees and his co-workers in the enterprise, were all his personal friends. One-half of them were his fellow-townsmen; and it so happened that a majority of them were Baptists, some of whom were leading clergymen and public educators of that denomination. This was an accidental result of his choice, occurring because Mr. Vassar's principal associates among men of learning were of that branch of the Christian Church, and was not a sign that the College would be, in any degree, specially influenced by men of any particular religious sect. And it is just praise of the institution to record, at the close of its second Collegiate year, that in the practical workings of its system of

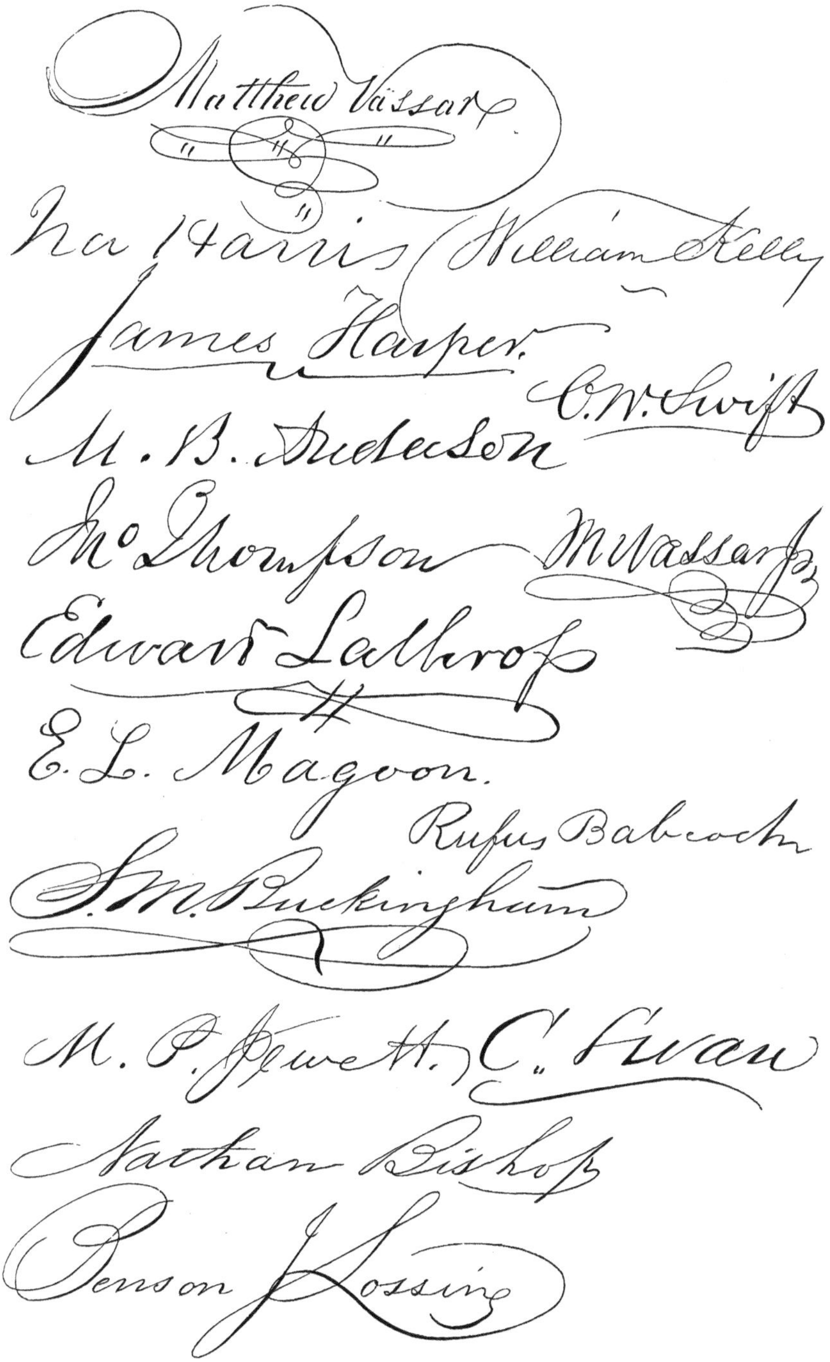

Matthew Vassar
" " "

Ira Harris

William Kelly

James Harper

C. W. Swift

M. B. Anderson

Jno Thompson

M. Vassar Jr

Edward Lathrop

E. L. Magoon.

Rufus Babcock

S. M. Buckingham

M. P. Jewett.

C. Swan

Nathan Bishop

Benson J. Lossing

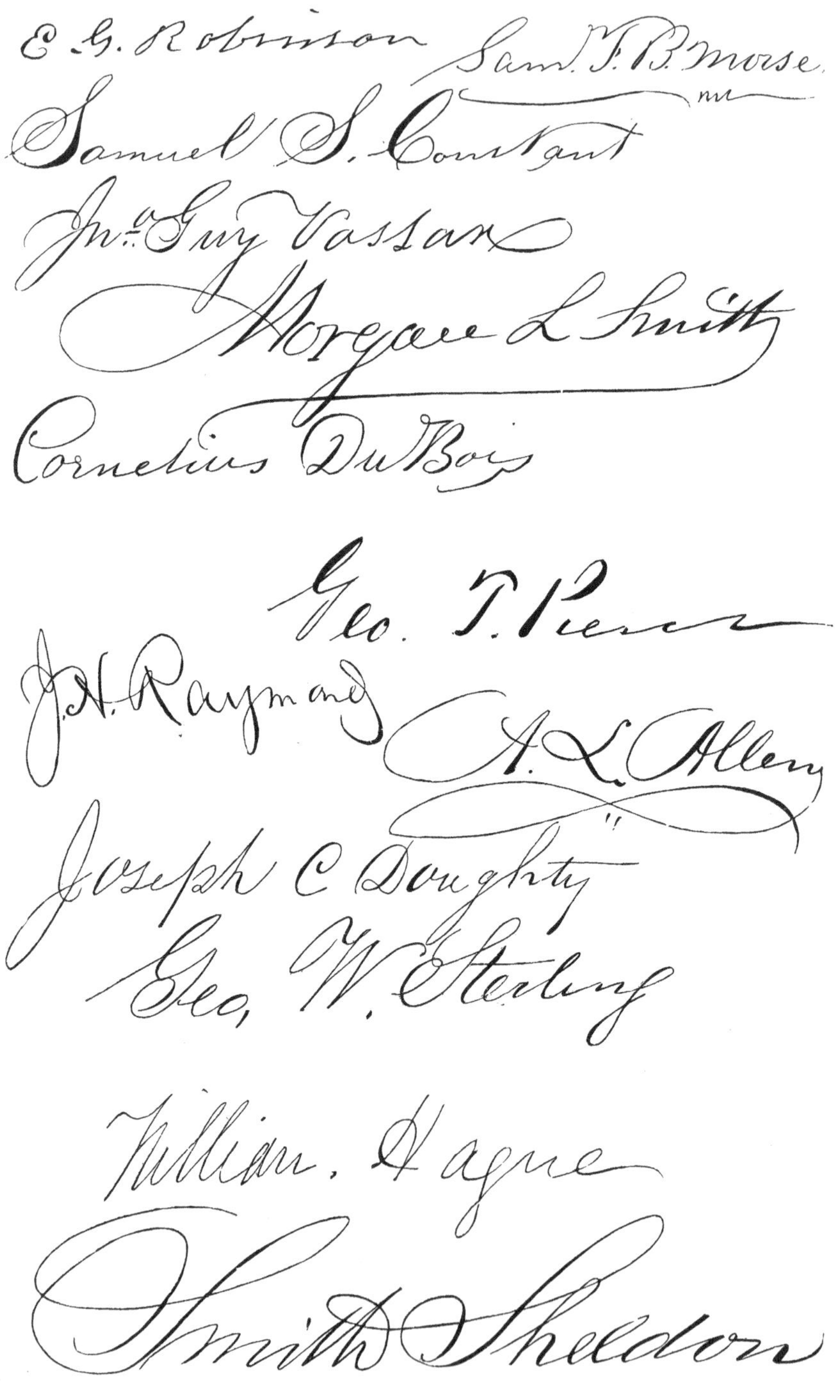

E. G. Robinson

Sam.l F. B. Morse

Samuel S. Constant

Jno. Guy Vassar

Morgan L. Smith

Cornelius DuBois

Geo. T. Pierce

J. H. Raymond

A. L. Allen

Joseph C. Doughty

Geo. W. Sterling

William. Hague

Smith Sheldon

education and moral and religious training, the pupils might never know, from their teachings alone, to what denomination of the Christian Church the Professors and Tutors belong.

Immediately after the act of incorporation became a law, Mr. Vassar, over his own signature, informed the several persons named in the Charter of the fact, and of their appointment; and they were requested to meet for the purpose of organizing a Board of Trustees, and adopting measures for carrying forward the great enterprise. They assembled, pursuant to public notice, in the parlor of the Gregory (now Morgan) House, in the city of Poughkeepsie, on the 26th of February, 1861. After a prayer by the Reverend Edward Lathrop, D. D., of New York City, a Board of Trustees was organized, by the election of the Honorable William Kelly, Chairman, and Cyrus Swan, Secretary. When this result was announced, Matthew Vassar, the Founder of the College, arose and read to the Trustees the following statement of his views and wishes:

"GENTLEMEN:—As my long-cherished purpose—to apply a large portion of my estate to some benevolent object—is now about to be accomplished, it seems proper that I should submit to you a statement of my motives, views, and wishes.

"It having pleased God that I should have no descendants to inherit my property, it has long been my desire, after suitably providing for those of my kindred who have claims on me, to make such a disposition of my means as should best honor God and benefit my fellow-men. At different periods I have regarded various plans with favor, but these have all been dismissed one after another, until the SUBJECT OF ERECTING AND ENDOWING A COLLEGE FOR THE EDUCATION OF YOUNG WOMEN was presented for my consideration. The novelty, grandeur, and benignity of the idea arrested my attention. The more carefully I examined it, the more strongly it commended itself to my judgment and interested my feelings.

"It occurred to me, that woman, having received from her Creator the same intellectual constitution as man, has the same right as man to intellectual culture and development.

"I considered that the MOTHERS of a country mold the character of its citizens, determine its institutions, and shape its destiny.

"Next to the influence of the mother, is that of the FEMALE TEACHER, who is employed to train young children at a period when impressions are most vivid and lasting.

"It also seemed to me, that if woman were properly educated, some new avenues to useful and honorable employment, in entire harmony with the gentleness and modesty of her sex, might be opened to her.

"It further appeared, there is not in our country, there is not in the world, so far as is known, a single fully endowed institution for the education of women.

"It was also in evidence that, for the last thirty years, the standard of education for the sex has been constantly rising in the United States; and the great, felt, pressing want has been ample endowments, to secure to Female Seminaries the elevated character, the stability and permanency of our best Colleges.

"And now, gentlemen, influenced by these and similar considerations, after devoting my best powers to the study of the subject for a number of years past; after duly weighing the objections against it, and the arguments that preponderate in its favor; and the project having received the warmest commendations of many prominent literary men and practical educators, as well as the universal approval of the public press, I have come to the conclusion, that the establishment and endowment of a College for the education of young women is a work which will satisfy my highest aspirations, and will be, under God, a rich blessing to this city and State, to our country and the world.

"It is my hope to be the instrument, in the hands of Providence, of founding and perpetuating an Institution which shall accomplish for young women what our colleges are accomplishing for young men.

"In pursuance of this design, I have obtained from the Legislature an act of incorporation, conferring on the proposed Seminary the corporate title of 'Vassar Female College,' and naming you, gentlemen, as the first Trustees. Under the provisions of this charter you are invested with all the powers, privileges, and immunities which appertain to any College or University in this State.

"To be somewhat more specific in the statement of my views as to the character and aims of the College:

"I wish that the course of study should embrace at least the following particulars: The English Language and its Literature; other Modern Languages; the Ancient Classics, so far as may be demanded by the spirit of the times; the Mathematics, to such an extent as may be deemed advisable; all the branches of Natural Science, with full apparatus, cabinets, collections, and conservatories for visible illustration; Anatomy, Physiology, and Hygiene, with practical reference to the laws of the health of the sex; Intellectual Philosophy; the elements of Political Economy; some knowledge of the Federal and State Constitutions and Laws; Moral Science, particularly as bearing on the filial, conjugal, and parental relations; Æsthetics, as treating of the beautiful in Nature and Art, and to be illustrated by an extensive Gallery of Art; Domestic Economy, practically taught, so far as is possible, in order to prepare the graduates readily to become skillful housekeepers; last, and most important of all, the daily, systematic Reading and Study of the Holy Scriptures, as the only and all-sufficient Rule of Christian faith and practice.

"All sectarian influences should be carefully excluded; but the training of our students should never be intrusted to the skeptical, the irreligious, or the immoral.

"In forming the first Board of Trustees, I have selected representatives from the principal Christian denominations among us; and in filling the vacancies which may occur in this body, as also in appointing the Professors, Teachers, and other Officers of the College, I trust a like catholic spirit will always govern the Trustees.

"It is not my purpose to make VASSAR FEMALE COLLEGE a charity school, whose advantages shall be free to all without charge; for benefits so cheaply obtained are cheaply held; but it is believed the funds of the Institution will enable it to offer to all the highest educational facilities at a moderate expense, as compared with the cost of instruction in existing seminaries. I earnestly hope the funds will also prove sufficient to warrant the gratuitous admission of a considerable number of indigent students, annually—at least, by regarding the amount remitted, in most cases, as a loan, to be subsequently repaid from the avails of teaching, or otherwise. Preference should be given to beneficiaries of decided promise—such as are likely to distinguish themselves in some particular department or pursuit—and, especially, to those who propose to engage in the teaching of the young as a profession.

"I desire that the College may be provided with commodious buildings, containing ample apartments for public instruction, and at the same time affording to the inmates the safety, quiet, privacy, and purity of the family.

"And now, gentlemen of the Board of Trustees, I transfer to your possession and ownership the real and personal property which I have set apart for the accomplishment of my designs."

While Mr. Vassar was reading this statement, he stood at the end of a table at which sat the Chairman and Secretary of the Board of Trustees. Near him, on the table, was a small tin box, which contained the funds appropriated for the founding of the College, represented by bonds and mortgages, certificates of stock, and a deed of conveyance of two hundred acres of land for a College site and farm. When he pronounced the last sentence above quoted, the Trustees arose. Mr. Vassar had placed his left hand on the precious casket, and, with its key in the open palm of his right hand, he then formally transferred from his own custody to that of the Trustees, more than four hundred thousand dollars of his wealth.

Who shall estimate the importance or measure the

significance of that act? Considered in its relations to society and to human selfishness, it was a moral spectacle of uncommon grandeur. Few men have lived who, after toiling half a century under the burden of great cares in gathering a large fortune, have dared to be so disloyal to ever-getting Human Nature as to lay down one-half of it on the altar of Benevolence, as a sacrifice for the sake of human needs. It was a revolutionary manifesto, declaring that the unrighteousness of the Paganism which has so long kept woman in bonds should yield to the justice of Christianity, whose Golden Rule makes her "free and equal" with Man.

Having performed that great act, Mr. Vassar said:—

"I beg permission to add a brief and general expression of my views in regard to the most judicious use and management of the funds. After the College edifice has been erected, and furnished with all needful aids and appliances for imparting the most perfect education of body, mind, and heart, it is my judgment and wish that the amount remaining in hand should be safely invested—to remain as a principal, only the annual income of which should be expended in the preservation of the buildings and grounds; the support of the faculty; the replenishing and enlarging of the library, cabinet, art gallery, etc., and in adding to the capital on hand; so that the college, instead of being impoverished, and tending to decay from year to year, shall always contain within itself the elements of growth and expansion, of increasing power, prosperity, and usefulness.

"In conclusion, gentlemen, this enterprise, which I regard as the last great work of my life, I commit to you as a sacred trust, which I feel assured you will discharge with fidelity and uprightness, with wisdom and prudence, with ability and energy.

"It is my fervent desire that I may live to see the Institution in successful operation; and, if God shall give me life and strength, I shall gladly employ my best faculties in co-operating with you to secure the full and perfect consummation of the work before us."

When Mr. Vassar and the Trustees resumed their seats, the Rev. Dr. Hague offered the following resolutions:—

"*Resolved*, That we, as Trustees, accept the munificent donation now presented by Matthew Vassar, Esq., for the purpose of founding and endowing Vassar Female College;

"That we highly appreciate the practical wisdom, the patriotic forecast, as well as the unparalleled liberality, which prompt him to devote so large a portion of his fortune to this noble work while he yet lives;

"That we pledge ourselves to use our best endeavors so to guard, foster, and apply these funds intrusted to us, as to fulfill his instructions and to realize his beneficent design;

"That the statement of Mr. Vassar's views just submitted be placed on the records of this Board; and also be engrossed on parchment, and preserved among the archives of the College forever."

Dr. Hague then said:—

"In offering these resolutions to the acceptance of this Board of Trustees, it may be proper for me to say a few words, expressive of my convictions as to the nature, the dignity, and the scope of the great trust that is now committed to our hands.

"The statements that have just been read by Mr. Vassar, unfolding his cherished aims in relation to the establishment of a Female College in this city, the munificence of his provisions, and the breadth of his plan, signalize an important step of progress in the advancement of intellectual culture throughout this country. It is adapted to call forth the sympathetic regards of the whole people in this sisterhood of States; for if there be any one feature that particularly distinguishes our American civilization in the view of the world, it is the influence of cultivated womanhood in the formation and development of American character.

"The power of this influence has been recognized by all careful observers, both at home and abroad. It has attracted the attention of tourists, philosophers, historians, and writers of every class. The most truthful, touching, and sincere eulogium that was ever uttered by an English author, as a tribute of honor to this country, came from the pen of an eminent prelate, Bishop Wilson (the successor of the celebrated Heber at Calcutta), when he declared that the American women, the wives of missionaries, whom he had had occasion to observe in Asia for a course of years, realized his best conceptions of cultivated Christian womanhood, of gentleness and refinement of manners, combined with the highest qualities of heroic excellence.

"This spontaneous tribute to the character of American women in our own age is in happy keeping with the most trusted testimonies of the past, in regard to the influence of that array of noble-minded women who had a conspicuous part to act in the training of this nation during the stormy days of its infancy, and thus in shaping our national destiny: a mighty moral force, that was pithily expressed by one of the officers of the French army at the close of the Revolutionary War, when, as Mr. Custis says, at a farewell entertainment given to them in Virginia, after having paid their respects to the mother of Washington, he exclaimed as she retired from the assembly-room, leaning on the arm of her son: 'No wonder that America has had such a leader, since he has had such a mother!'

"Those were times, Mr. Chairman, that subjected womanly character to the most searching ordeals, and developed all its latent energies. The men who were engrossed by the demands of public affairs were obliged to leave the education of their sons almost entirely to the mother at home. A fine exemplification of this is furnished in the letters of President Adams to his wife in regard to their domestic concerns, and especially the education of their son, John Quincy Adams, whose name now shines as a brilliant star in the firmament of American history. The letters of Mrs. Adams to her son prove her high qualifications for the discharge of her sacred trust; and the long, arduous lifework of that eminent man is to be regarded, in part, as her own cherished legacy to the land that she loved, and to the generation which is now in the prime of its manly power, as well as to that which has already passed away.

"And here I am naturally led to remark that the sentiment which has just now been expressed, in the written statement that Mr. Vassar has presented to us, is fully verified by all the teachings of our national history. He speaks of the necessity of providing such an education for the females of this country as shall be adequate to give them a position of intellectual *equality* with men, in domestic and social life. The thought looms up with new aspects of dignity, the more closely it is considered. In olden times, this equality was a marked feature of American life, manners, and habits. The wife was not merely the superintendent of a household: she was the honored friend, companion, and counselor. In the settlement of these colonies, more than two centuries ago, she was the sharer not only of domestic joys and sorrows, but of all the cares pertaining to the establishment of the Church, the State, and the nation. Then the sons and daughters of America were educated together, and their attainments were so nearly alike as to constitute a social equipoise, that for a long period continued firm and undisturbed. But of late years, the wealth and energies of the people have been lavished upon colleges and universities for young men to such an extent in this one line of direction, that the balance is no longer even, and the former adjustment of the social forces has become somewhat deranged. This derangement must be remedied, the balance must be restored, or our national character cannot hold its place of eminence, but must gravitate toward an abyss. If the time shall come when the educated young men of America shall cease to look up to their mothers with the sentiments of respect that were cherished by our fathers in their young days, if our sons shall cease to find in their sisters companions suited to their mental needs, home-life must lose its former attractions; the moral atmosphere that has surrounded the household will be no longer genial; and the most fearful organic evils that have been inherent in the social structure of many nations in the Old World will be reproduced on our soil in rank luxuriance, and with consequences that enfold a vast and irremediable ruin.

"It was not without good reason that a distinguished American traveler in Turkey said, that he despaired of any valid reformation of that once strong but now decaying nation, until woman should be restored to that position of social equality that God had originally assigned to her; and it was with equal reason that a French statesman declared, many years ago, that 'the chief want of France is mothers!' So, too, we may rest assured that the great work to which American patriotism is now called to task itself, is that of sustaining and extending the influence of a well-cultivated Christian womanhood throughout the length and breadth of these United States, which we all love to call 'our country,' and whose citizenship has so long been the shield of our safety, honor, and prosperity.

"With these views, Mr. Chairman, I submit the resolutions now before you."

The resolutions offered by Dr. Hague were adopted by the unanimous vote of the Trustees. Then Matthew Vassar, Jr., a nephew of the Founder, was chosen to be the Treasurer of the Board, and the title-deeds and assignments, duly executed, which had been absolutely and unconditionally given to Vassar College, were placed in his custody.

The choice of President of the College followed this provision for the administration of its funds; and Professor Milo P. Jewett, who had rendered such signal service in the inception and growth of the enterprise, was by unanimous vote chosen to fill that important station. The chairman then proceeded to nominate the following Standing Committees for the ensuing year:

Executive Committee.

Charles W. Swift, Matthew Vassar, Jr.,
Matthew Vassar, Cyrus Swan,
Cornelius Dubois.

On the Faculty and Studies.

Milo P. Jewett, John H. Raymond,
Martin B. Anderson, Edward G. Robinson,
Nathan Bishop, Rufus Babcock.

On the Library.

Rufus Babcock, James Harper,
Ira Harris, William Hague,
Edward Lathrop, Smith Sheldon.

On Cabinets and Apparatus.

Martin B. Anderson, George T. Pierce,
Morgan L. Smith, Stephen M. Buckingham,
Edward G. Robinson.

On the Art Gallery.

ELIAS L. MAGOON, BENSON J. LOSSING,
SAMUEL F. B. MORSE, JOHN THOMPSON,
JOHN GUY VASSAR.

On Building and Grounds.

MATTHEW VASSAR, JOSEPH C. DOUGHTY,
CORNELIUS DUBOIS, AUGUSTUS L. ALLEN,
S. S. CONSTANT.

On Corporation Seal.

MILO P. JEWETT, BENSON J. LOSSING, GEORGE W. STERLING.

On By-laws.

GEORGE T. PIERCE, CHARLES W. SWIFT, CYRUS SWAN.

Immediately after the organization of the Board of Trustees, measures were adopted for erecting the College building, without delay. The plans of Mr. Tefft were not used. He went to Europe soon after completing them, for the purpose of increasing his professional knowledge. He had proposed that nothing should be done toward the erection of a college building until after his return, as he hoped to bring with him important information that might enable him to make essential improvements in his plan. Mr. Vassar's acquiescence was readily given, and presented another instance of the great deliberation with which the Founder acted at that time, and to which allusion has been made.

Mr. Tefft died at Florence, in Italy, and James Renwick, Jr., the architect of the edifice of the Smithsonian Institute, in Washington City, was employed to make plans and specifications for a college building commensurate with the Founder's liberal designs. These were laid before the Board at the time of its organization, and were accepted. The Executive Committee of the Board soon afterward made a contract with Mr. Renwick for the erection of an edifice in accordance with those plans, and with William Harloe as the builder.

The college site and farm conveyed to the Trustees by the Founder lies nearly two miles eastward of the

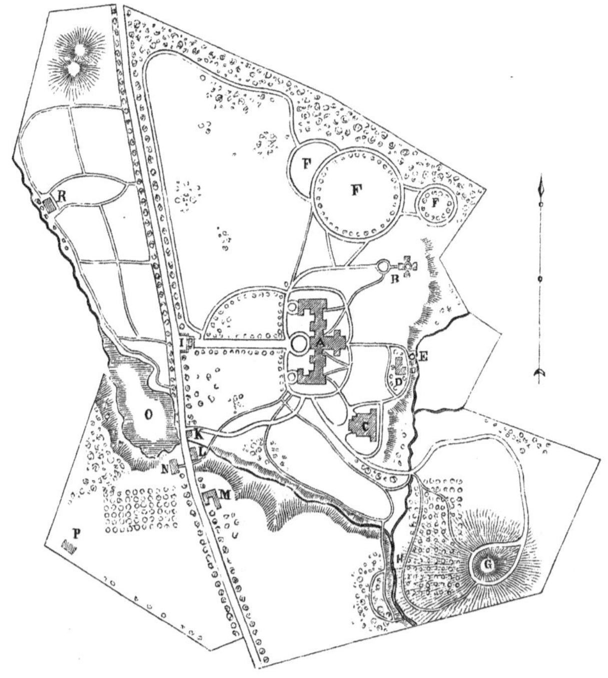

Court-House in Poughkeepsie, and at a little greater distance from the Hudson River. Its boundary and superficial lines are irregular, as the accompanying map*

* This map is from surveys made by the first class in Trigonometry that was formed in Vassar College. The localities are indicated as follows:

A. College.
B. Observatory.
C. Gymnasium.
D. Gas and Boiler House.
E. Gasometer.
F. Play-grounds.
G. Sunset Hill.
H. Casper's Kill.
I. Gate and Porter's Lodge.
K. Pump-house.
R. Garden Store-house.
L. Ice-house.
M. Barn and Stable.
N. Farm-house.
O. Mill-cove Lake.
P. Tenant-house.

shows, and presents at many points beautiful landscape effects, near and remote. Not far from its eastern border, and between it and the village of Manchester, rises a lofty hill, to the top of which Mr. Vassar's elder sister sometimes took him, when he was a child six or eight years of age, that he might be gratified with a sight of the two church steeples in Poughkeepsie. And over the little stream that crosses the highway near by, and flows through the eastern portions of the college grounds, he had often passed with his mother, on a rude bridge half hidden by the luxuriant calamus or sweet-flag. Had some venerated seer then predicted that in the morning shadows of that hill the little English boy would one day build a magnificent palace of learning, and along that little stream would be seen groups of young women, gathered from every part of the Great Republic of the West, enjoying the blessings of his munificence, the most credulous admirer of the prophet would have refused belief in the prophecy.

A site for the college edifice on the bank of the river seemed more desirable than one so inland; but, when both were carefully considered, the advantages offered by the one chosen were manifestly greater than any to be found on the Hudson, near Poughkeepsie. It was far enough away from those great lines of travel, the river and the railway, which afford facilities for a multitude of intrusions and annoyances, to avoid the latter altogether, and was sufficiently near the city to make its markets and merchandise easily available. It was in a healthful place, in the midst of beautiful rural scenery, with much of the horizon bounded by distant mountains. More desirable than any thing else, for the health and

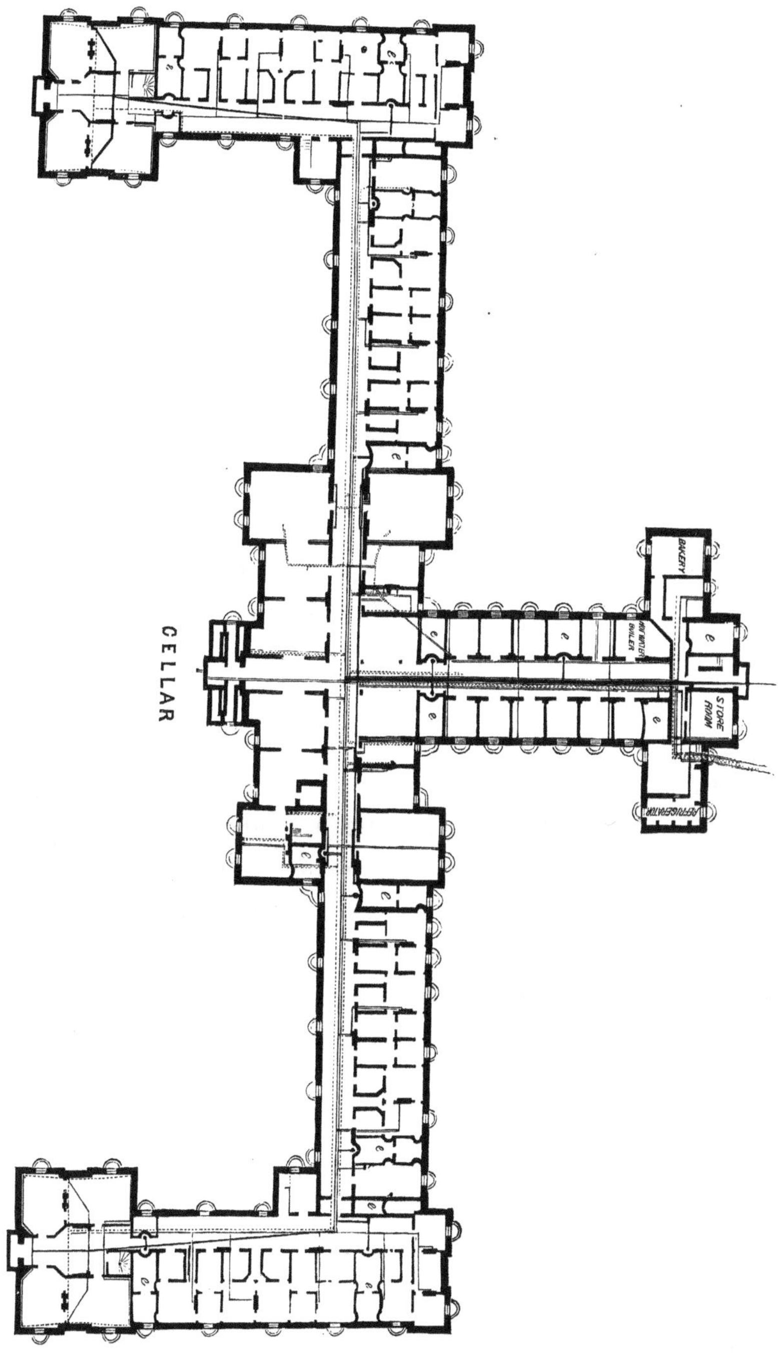
CELLAR
BAKERY
STORE ROOM

comfort of the inmates of the projected college, was a large pond of pure spring water on the grounds, whose fountains had never failed in their abundance, and whose outlet, that had for years turned a mill-wheel, presented an assurance that an all-bountiful supply would be given.

The site on the farm selected for the College building was a little plain, bounded on the west by the highway, and on the east and south by a ravine and gentle hollows. It was once the Duchess County Race-Course, and was without tree or shrub. There the outlines of the edifice were marked out by the architect and builder; and on Tuesday, the 4th day of June, 1861, Mr. Vassar "broke ground" there with his own strength. Only two of the Trustees (Messrs. Du Bois and Swan), the Reverend Howard Malcom, D. D., of Philadelphia, Mr. Sipher the farmer, and one or two others, were present on that beautiful Summer morning, as witnesses of the interesting ceremonial. At the request of the Founder, Dr. Malcom, in a brief supplication, asked God's blessing on the enterprise. Then Mr. Vassar, thrusting a spade into the ground, lifted almost a cubic foot of earth from its bed, at the point where the trench that was to receive the foundation stones of the building was to begin. The farmer then placed his plow there, with which he was to furrow the outline of the trench, and this Mr. Vassar held for some distance on its prescribed course. The form of that outline may be seen by reference to the ground-plan of the College building on the preceding page, which shows the relative position of all the foundation walls on which the superstructure is built, from the ground to the roof. A more particular reference to this cellar-plan will be made hereafter.

So it was, wholly without ostentatious display, and with the simple religious ceremony of prayer to God, in the presence of a few of his fellow-citizens, that the Founder of Vassar College, with his own hands, began the material labor of the enterprise. That spadeful of earth was placed in a jar, and, with the implement with which it was raised, it is preserved, as a precious memorial, in the Geological Cabinet of the College.

The late Civil War was kindling when the Board of Trustees of Vassar College was organized. Already, State Conventions in seven of the Commonwealths of the Republic had declared the withdrawal of those States from the Union; and representatives from these in convention at Montgomery, in Alabama, had formed a provisional constitution for a League known as the Confederate States of America. To the apprehension of the wisest and most hopeful, the immediate future of the country appeared exceedingly gloomy. Civil War, with all its calamities, seemed inevitable. The shocks of the political earthquake then rocking the nation to its center were rapidly unsettling all values, and some of the securities which formed a part of the College fund seemed worthless. But the Founder and the Trustees went steadily forward in the great work, at that time and during the entire period of the terrible war that ensued; and in the month succeeding the cessation of hostilities, the Board, at its annual meeting (June, 1865), found the College edifice so nearly completed and equipped, its system of instruction so well planned, and the appointments to the chairs of professorships so satisfactorily made, that it was determined to announce that the Institution would be opened for the reception of students early in the ensuing Autumn. The

College fund had been so well managed by the Treasurer of the Board that it had not been diminished, excepting by the necessary expenditures.

At the first annual meeting of the Board of Trustees, on the 25th of February, 1862, the President of the College asked leave of absence, for the purpose of studying the systems of education prevailing in the most enlightened countries of Europe, and especially those for the instruction of young women, with the view of advancing the interests of the Institution over which he was to preside. That leave was given; and the President was requested to prepare, while abroad, a general and statistical report on the subject, in which he should compare the systems in Europe with those in use in our country, and to make to the Board such suggestions as should seem to him worthy of its attention.

President Jewett embarked for England on the 5th of April, 1862, and arrived in London on the 19th of the same month. Through the agency of the United States Minister at the Court of St. James, many facilities for the prosecution of his errand were afforded him. He spent several weeks in London, visiting its educational establishments for both sexes; scientific and other institutions; galleries of art; manufactories of philosophical instruments; libraries, and other helps to knowledge; and in every way seeking useful hints for the benefit of Vassar College. He was treated with respect and courtesy, for the novel enterprise which he represented commanded the most profound attention wherever it was made known; and it was frequently mentioned in connection with the then recent gift of a large sum of money to the city of London, by the eminent American banker, George Peabody, for the benefit of the poor of that metropolis.

After visiting the Universities of Oxford and Cambridge, and schools for girls in other parts of Great Britain, the President crossed the Channel and spent three weeks in Paris, in the business of the same errand. Most of the schools for young women in that city were conventual Seminaries, in which religious instruction and duties were prominent features, and could afford but few valuable hints to an American educator. Through the kindness of the Embassador of the Republic at the Court of St. Cloud, he obtained an audience with the French Minister of Public Instruction, who gave him many facilities for the prosecution of his inquiries. From Paris he went to Berlin, Vienna, Dresden, Munich, and other European capitals; and, after visiting Rome and other cities in Italy, he returned home.

In a Report to the Board of Trustees, at their next annual meeting (June, 1863), the President gave an account of his journey abroad, and a summary of his observations concerning the education of girls and young women. He observed that great prominence was given to religious instruction, especially in the schools in Germany: that the pupils were almost universally taught orally, especially in Prussia, by which they obtained ideas instead of words only: that domestic economy received much attention, especially in the schools connected with the nunneries on the Continent, and in the training schools for young women in Great Britain: that special attention was given to the bodily health of the pupils, by systematic exercise in the open air, and by calisthenics, dancing, and other healthful in-door movements, which promote physical vigor, and ease and grace in motion: that extreme plainness and simplicity of diet, and also of dress, was a general rule in Great Britain and on the Continent; and that in many institutions there was a uniformity in dress, the garments being made of subdued colors, while laces and jewels were entirely discarded: that the cultivation of vocal and instrumental music was a prominent object of instruction: that dancing and painting also occupied a conspicuous place in all the schools; and that the study of modern languages was almost universal in them.

These special features of instruction, noticed by the President, appeared to him more perfect than the same in the schools of this country; yet he came to the conclusion that there could be but little learned, for use in American schools, from the *systems* abroad. There is, in many particulars, but a remote resemblance between those of our Republic and of Europe, for the obvious reason that each is fashioned in accordance with the demands of the political and social organizations by which it is fostered, and to which it is expected to conform. If the President did not bring back with him any positive wealth of knowledge to enrich the inchoate Seminary, he had observed the defects in foreign schools with sufficient distinctness and care to prevent their finding a place in the organization of the new Institution.

Leaving out of sight the peculiar systems of education in Europe, as such, and carefully considering those special features of training and instruction which they presented that seemed essentially useful, the Committee on Faculty and Studies proceeded to prepare a plan of organization, discipline, and course of teaching for the College, in accordance with the principles and requirements of our Republican institutions, the demands of our correlative social system, and the importance, manifest to every enlightened mind, of thoroughly educating the future mothers of this nation. They made an elaborate report of their labors to the Board of Trustees, at its annual meeting at the close of June, 1863, which was printed and distributed among the members of the Board, and educators throughout the country, that the College might have the benefit of their friendly criticisms.

The final organization of the College in all its departments for its great work will be described presently. Through all the years of preparation for that work, the Founder was not only a deeply interested spectator, but a most zealous co-worker. At every annual meeting of the Board, he opened its proceedings by reading a statement of his views and wishes, which were always listened to with the most profound attention; and these suggestions were acted upon as far as practicable. He especially desired the full co-operation of women in the labor of instruction and discipline in the College; and he was anxious that professors of her sex, if competent persons might be found, should form a part of the Faculty. So deeply was he impressed with the justice and policy of such an arrangement, that at the meeting in June, 1864, when the question of the appointment of professors was to be considered, he made the subject the topic of his regular discourse, in the course of which he said:

"It is my hope—it was my only hope and desire—indeed, it has been the main incentive to all I have already done, or may hereafter do, or hope to do, to inaugurate a new era in the history and life of woman. The attempt you are to aid me in making fails wholly of its point if it be not an advance, and a decided advance. I wish to give one sex all the advantages too long monopolized by the other. Ours is, and is to be, an institution for women—not men. In all its labors, positions, rewards, and hopes, the idea is the development and exposition, and the marshaling to the front and the preferment of women—of their powers on every side, demonstrative of their equality with men—demonstrative, indeed, of such capacities as in certain fixed directions surpass those of men. This, I conceive, may be fully accomplished within the rational limits of true womanliness, and without the slightest hazard to the attractiveness of her character. We are indeed already defeated before we commence, if such development be in the least dangerous to the dearest attributes of her sex. We are not the less defeated, if it be hazardous for her to avail herself of her highest educated powers when that point is gained. We are defeated if we start upon the assumption that she has no powers save those she may derive, or imitate, from the other sex. We are defeated if we recognize the idea that she may not, with every propriety, contribute to the world the benefits of matured faculties which education evokes. We are especially defeated if we fail to express, by our acts, our practical belief in her pre-eminent powers as an instructor of her own sex."

We have now observed the growth of one of the most remarkable and important of the world's seminaries of learning, from the germ of a suggestion, vivified by benevolent action, to almost maturity of form and capacity for bearing fruit. At the beginning of the year 1865, on that little plain where Mr. Vassar, less than four years earlier, cast up a spadeful of earth and plowed a simple furrow, the Vassar College building stood in all its grand proportions, external and internal. Near it had arisen, over the immovable foundation of a great rock, the walls and dome of an Astronomical Observatory, which had been erected under the skillful directions of Charles S. Farrar, A. M., who afterward became a member of the College Faculty, as Professor of Mathematics, Natural Philosophy, and Chemistry. In another direction, at the main entrance to the grounds, a stately Gateway and Porter's Lodge was a-building; and everywhere the sounds of industry were heard. When April came, the planting of trees and the forming of graveled walks and drives began to develop grace and symmetry here and there, that prophesied of the ultimate beauty of the domain in form and feature. When the Board of Trustees assembled, in June, the College building was almost ready for its equipment of furniture and apparatus. Then, as we have observed, it was determined to open it for the reception of pupils in the ensuing Autumn. The Summer was

GATEWAY AND PORTER'S LODGE.

spent in preparations for that event; and on the 20th day of September, 1865, the first collegiate year of Vassar College was begun.

So early as the Spring of 1864, circumstances had caused Dr. Jewett to offer his resignation of the Presidency of the College, and of trusteeship. It was accepted, and he was succeeded in the former office by John H. Raymond, LL. D., who was one of the Trustees, an active member of the Committee on Faculty and Studies, and a successful educator, of long experience. Dr. Jewett's place in the Board of Trustees was filled by Reverend Henry Ward Beecher. With this exception, the members of the Board, and also its officers, are the same as when it was organized, more than six years ago.

The work of the College was commenced by the following officers of government and instruction:—

JOHN H. RAYMOND, LL. D., President, and Professor of Mental and Moral Philosophy.

HANNAH W. LYMAN, Lady Principal.

WILLIAM I. KNAPP, A. M., Professor of Ancient and Modern Languages.

CHARLES S. FARRAR, A. M., Professor of Mathematics, Natural Philosophy, and Chemistry.

SANBORN TENNEY, A. M., Professor of Natural History, including Geology and Mineralogy, Botany, Zoölogy, and Physical Geography.

MARIA MITCHELL, Professor of Astronomy, and Director of the Observatory.

ALIDA C. AVERY, M. D., Professor of Physiology and Hygiene, and Resident Physician.

HENRY B. BUCKHAM, A. M., Professor of Rhetoric, Belles-lettres, and the English Language.

EDWARD WIEBÉ, Professor of Vocal and Instrumental Music.

HENRY VON INGEN, Professor of Drawing and Painting.

LOUIS F. RONDEL, Instructor in the French Language.

DELIA F. WOODS, Instructor in the Department of Physical Training.

JESSIE USHER, Teacher of the Latin Language.

LUCIA M. GILBERT, Teacher of the Greek Language.

PRISCILLA H. BRAISLIN, Teacher of Mathematics.

ELIZA M. WILEY, Teacher of Music.

EMMA SAYLES, Teacher of Chemistry, Mathematics, and the English Language.

SARAH L. WYMAN, Teacher of the Latin Language.

CAROLINE H. METCALF, Teacher of the French and English Languages.

BARBARA GRANT, Teacher of Mathematics and Chemistry.

KATE FESSENDEN, Teacher of the French Language.

SARAH E. SCOTT, Teacher of Rhetoric and Mathematics.

EMILY A. BRADDOCK, Teacher of the Latin Language.

MARY DASCOMB, Teacher of Mathematics.

JULIA WIEBÉ, Teacher of Music.

EMMA L. HOPKINS, Teacher of Music.

CAROLINE S. C. WIEBÉ, Teacher of Music.

SOPHIA L. CURTIS, Teacher of Music.

A. AMELIA JUDD, Teacher of Music.

FANNY J. SMALL, Teacher of Music.

THE GYMNASIUM.

Late in the year, and before the spacious Gymnasium, that now stands on a knoll south-eastward of the main edifice, was erected, classes for physical training had been organized and instructed in the corridors of the College building, by ELIZABETH M. POWELL (Miss Woods had left because of ill health), who continues to preside over that most important branch of education; and at the opening of the second collegiate year, when the Gymnasium was completed, its riding school was placed in charge of LEOPOLD VON SELDENECK, who was for a long time a cavalry officer in the Prussian army, and served in that capacity in our National army during the Civil War.

The auspicious beginning of Vassar College gave the Founder the most perfect satisfaction. The desire to have this result reached during his lifetime was gratified. With faith and hope, and yet with intense anxiety, he had labored with the Trustees (first as Chairman of the Committee on Building and Grounds, and then as presiding officer of the Executive Committee) until the Institution was ready to begin its work, when, as the following correspondence shows, he withdrew from further participation in the task of management:

"SPRINGSIDE, POUGHKEEPSIE, *June* 17, 1865.

"NATHAN BISHOP, LL. D.:

"MY DEAR SIR:—The first stage in the development of that great enterprise to which I have devoted a large portion of my fortune and the latest labors of my life, is now drawing to a close. The erection of the College edifice, and its equipment with the material apparatus of instruction, will soon be completed; and, with the coming Autumn, its interior life as a great educational establishment will begin.

"Thus far the great work of the Executive Committee has been, in a great measure, that of a building committee, and I have cheerfully shared its perplexities and toils, from a conviction that my long experience in the management of material affairs would enable me to give them important aid.

"Although a kind Providence has blessed me with more than ordinary health and vigor for my years, yet I begin to feel sensibly the wear and tear of these numerous and ever-multiplying details; and since the business of the Executive Committee must hereafter pertain more than heretofore to the internal regulation of the College, I have felt a strong desire to be relieved by some gentleman, who, in addition to the general qualities of business capacity, high probity, and public spirit, possesses a special experience and practical knowledge in the management of an institution of learning.

"With this view, I have not only looked carefully over the list of our Trustees, but extended my view through the entire range of my acquaintance, and, among all within my reach, or *beyond* my reach, I find no one who possesses those qualifications so eminently and so entirely as yourself. It is my desire, therefore, at the approaching meeting of the Board of Trustees, to resign my present place as chairman of the Executive Committee; and my earnest hope is that you will consent to accept and discharge this honorable trust.

"I have requested President Raymond, and our mutual friend, Mr. Stephen M. Buckingham, to be the bearers of this communication, and to give any further explanation of my views (of which they are fully informed), that you may desire.

"Meanwhile, believe me, dear Sir,

"Yours very respectfully, &c.,

"M. VASSAR."

"NEW YORK, *June* 23, 1865.

"MATTHEW VASSAR, ESQ.:

"MY DEAR SIR:—Yesterday President Raymond and S. M. Buckingham, Esq., presented me your kind letter of the 21st inst.

"After a somewhat full conversation with them, I consented to comply with your request. In taking this step I have yielded my own preferences to your wishes, for I assure you that it has long been a source of pleasure to me to co-operate with you in establishing Vassar Female College—an institution which will become a perpetual blessing to the country, and place you among the great benefactors of mankind.

"With best regards,

"I remain, dear Sir,

"Very truly yours,

"NATHAN BISHOP."

Let us now consider the College buildings, and their equipment and uses, which in their present complete state have cost a little more than half a million of dollars.

The main edifice, whose outward appearance is seen on page 11, and its ground-plan on page 101, is almost five hundred feet in length, with a breadth through the center of about two hundred feet, and at the transverse wings of one hundred and sixty-four feet. It is constructed of dull red brick, the joints pointed with black mortar. The water-tables, and trimmings of the doors and windows, are made of blue free-stone. The center building and the wings are five stories in height, and the connecting portions are four stories in height. Within the edifice are five independent dwellings for resident officers; accommodations for about four hundred students; apartments for a full complement of managers and servants; suits of rooms for class recitations, lectures, and instruction in music and painting; a chapel; dining hall; parlors;

suitable apartments for a library and art gallery, philosophical apparatus, laboratories, cabinets of Natural History, and all other appurtenances of a first-class college. Also ample arrangements for a kitchen, bakery, and laundry.

The height of the center building, from the foundation to the top of the dome, is ninety-two feet. All of the partition walls are of brick, and are carried up from the ground to the roof. There is a corridor in each story, twelve feet in width and five hundred and eighty-five feet in length, affording room for exercise in inclement weather. These corridors may be instantly divided into five separate parts, by iron doors connected with eight fire-proof walls. The latter are in pairs, standing ten feet apart, and cut the building into five divisions. These pairs of walls are connected only at the corridors, where the floor is brick and stone, over which the iron doors may slide and be closed, so that, should a conflagration occur in one portion of the building, the other parts would be perfectly secure from harm. These divisions of iron and masonry extend from the foundation to the roof.

For further security against accident by fire, iron pipes, from water-tanks on the attic floor, pass down through the different stories. To these hose is attached on each floor, and conveys water with great force. A steam or water pump may be instantly brought into use, if needed. There are but two fires kept in the College building; one for cooking, and one for heating flat-irons. A watchman traverses the building all night, and the engineer or his assistant is always on duty. There are nine stair-ways from the top to the bottom of the building (two of them fire-proof), and eight passages for egress. These several provisions seem to make the students absolutely secure from accidents by fire.

Over the entire building six thousand feet of lightning rods are spread, after the most approved and scientific methods used for defense against thunder-bolts, as the common phrase is; and running through it in all directions, and connecting with external points, are pipes for conveying gas, heat, water, and waste, about twenty-five miles in aggregate length.

Now let us go through the building, from the bottom to the top, and observe the arrangement, equipment, and uses of each floor.

Here is the cellar (see plan on page 101), traversed by the lower sections of all the pipes. In the eastern portion of the center are cisterns *e e e e*, and at its end are the refrigerator, store-room, bakery, and boiler. Little else is to be seen excepting the foundation walls; so we will go up from this gloomy place to the first story (whose plan is on the following page), where there is more light, air, and interest. The entrance is in the center building. On the right of the passage are rooms for the transaction of the general business of the College. The first is occupied by the Registrar and Clerk, and the adjoining one is the Trustees' Room, in which the Executive Committee meets, and the Treasurer and Secretary keep their books and papers. Adjoining this is the kitchen of the President's house (H).

On the left of the passage are three connecting rooms devoted to practical instruction in Chemistry. G is the Laboratory; C, a recitation-room; and A, a commodious lecture-room, twenty-five by thirty feet in area, and

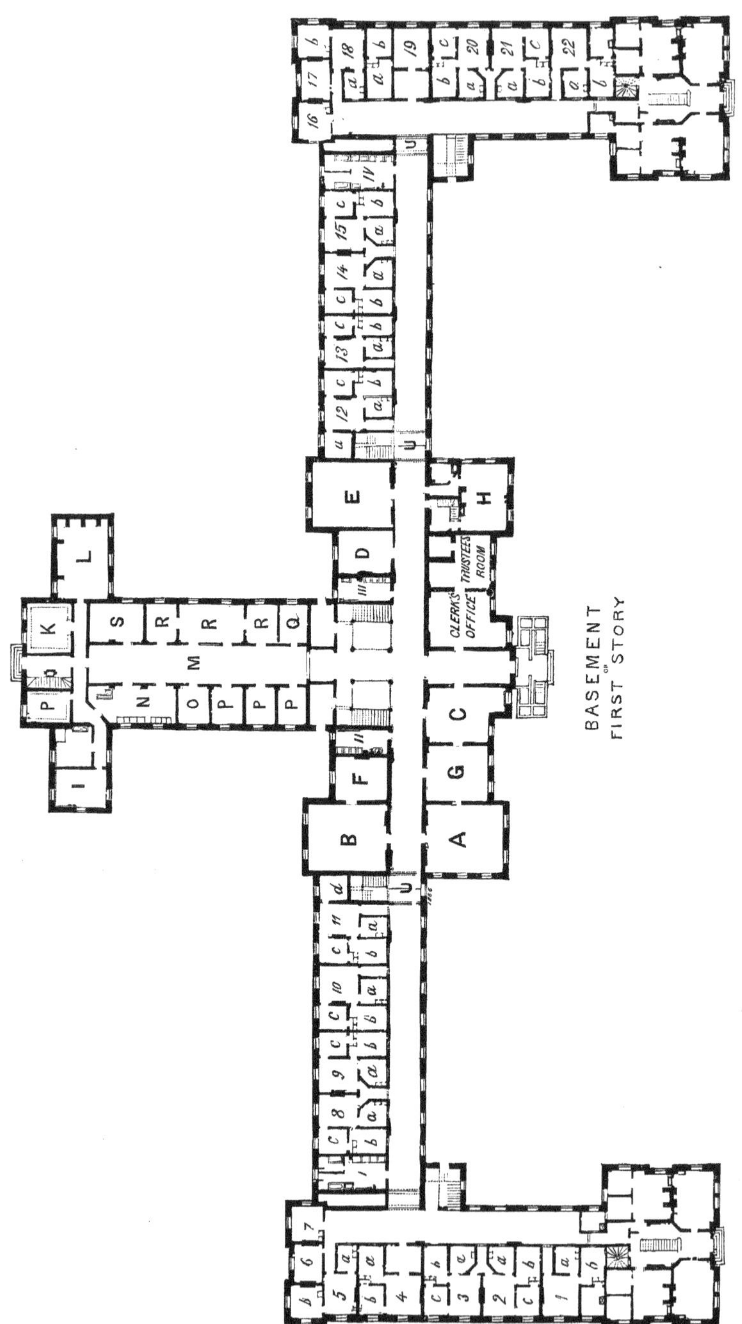
BASEMENT or FIRST STORY
CLERK'S OFFICE
TRUSTEES ROOM
A
B
C
D
E
F
G
H
I
K
L
M
N
O
P
Q
R
S
U

fifteen feet in height. It is seated in gallery style, and its walls are hung with portraits of Chemists most distinguished in the development of the science. These are made useful by familiarizing the students with their features and biography, and thus teaching the history of chemistry, and increasing the learners' interest in the study. The Laboratory and Lecture-rooms were planned and furnished with apparatus and materials with special reference to practice by the students in the elements of the science. Most of the apparatus was imported directly for the College, and is of the most perfect kind. Here is a hooded sink and a hooded table; there, in the center, is a testing-table; yonder in a corner is a furnace and spacious hearth; and at proper places are gas and water conveniences. Here the student not only learns, but investigates, and so her information becomes knowledge. She may here demonstrate the fact that in a drop of water there is sufficient latent electricity, as the philosophers express it, to give the phenomena of a thunderstorm; and so she may explain the moral potency of woman's tears, that has been felt ever since our common Mother regained the paradise of her husband's affections by the key that opened the celestial gate to the Peri, when the penitent Wife,

> "with tears that ceased not flowing,
> And tresses all disordered, at his feet
> Fell humble, and in Adam wrought
> Commiseration."

Let us cross the corridor and pass into the lecture-room of the Natural Philosophy Department (B), wherein the student is taught how to explore the mysteries of nature in broader fields. This room is of the same dimensions as that of the Chemistry Department, is seated in the same way, and furnished with conveniences for the uses of instruction. On its walls are portraits of eminent Philosophers; and in a smaller room adjoining (F) are the philosophical instruments of the Còllege. The supply of apparatus is not large, but well selected, and each perfect of its kind. The plan of the Professor of this Department is not to have instruments for mere illustration, for which the Black-board is better adapted, but to have them all such as may serve the purposes of investigation as well as illustration, believing that a little actual research is more valuable training in science than mere learning. This age of experiments and wholesome infidelity to theories continually demands new modifications and new varieties of instruments; and such are constantly added to the collection in Vassar College. Here in this little room may be seen some of the most interesting implements used in scientific investigations by modern explorers. Among these is the apparatus of pendulum and indicator, by which Faucoult has recently demonstrated the fact of the rotary motion of the earth, and by which his experiments were successfully repeated at Vassar College, on the night of the 18th of March, 1867, by Professor Farrar and his class. The pendulum ball then used was a sphere of lead, weighing forty-six pounds. It was suspended from the roof of the College building, by a wire sixty-four feet in length, over the open space within the north central stairway, and was made to vibrate over a carefully graduated circle of three feet in diameter. Problems of the pendulum had been previously worked out by the class, and the experiment verified the correctness of their calculations. The plane of oscillation was found to rotate nearly at the rate of ten degrees an hour, which is the rate demanded for the latitude of the College (41° 40′ 50″), on the hypothesis of the daily rotation of the earth on its axis. This incident is mentioned as an illustration of the fact that every new experiment and demonstration in science is brought to the practical notice of the students of Vassar College.

Pages might be filled with a catalogue and description of the philosophical instruments, but we may notice only one or two more, and then pass on to other apartments. Look at that modest little mahogany box, with a row of small discs on the top, like the finger-keys of an accordion. Here is a little crank. How easily it turns! Put your finger on that button. You are startled! And well you may be, for there is a giant in that box, terrible in its anger, but harmless when unprovoked. It is of a race once employed to strike mortal blows at the life of the Republic; now it is occasionally engaged in the more peaceful labor of decomposing water. It is one of Wheatstone's improved Magneto-Electric Machines, that was used in Charleston Harbor, during the late Civil War, for exploding floating mines of gunpowder, called torpedoes, under National vessels.

Here are some beautiful instruments, used by Tyndall in his recent delicate experiments and demonstrations concerning the nature of heat, light, and motion, which threaten to greatly modify all previous theories on those subjects. These seem to open to the human understanding deeper knowledge of the Universe,

"Whose body Nature is, and God the soul;"

and lead us to a more comprehensive idea of that

subtle, all-pervading, and mysterious emanation from the Omnipotent, which, as Pope said, more than a century ago,

> "Warms in the sun, refreshes in the breeze,
> Glows in the stars, and blossoms in the trees;
> Lives through all life, extends through all extent,
> Spreads undivided, operates unspent."

It would be delightful to linger here among these revelators of the mysteries of the Universe; but we must pass on to places and things of more personal importance to tutors and students. Before doing so, let us spend a few minutes in the Natural History Laboratory (D), and Recitation-room (E), in which may be found specimens in abundance of the products of the three kingdoms whose history and character are here studied; also illustrative maps, diagrams, and drawings. In connection with the studies in this department, which include the subjects of Geology, Physical Geography, Botany, Mineralogy, and Zoölogy, the cabinets belonging to the College, and situated upon other floors, are freely used. Much study is also performed in the woods and fields, when the weather permits.

There is a syllogism as old as the creation, that may run thus: All mortal creatures must eat and sleep; human beings are mortal; therefore, human beings, like gazelles and birds of paradise, must eat and sleep. In compliance with this truth, ample provision is made in Vassar College for the sustenance and repose of its inmates. Look along this corridor, on the floor we are exploring, and you will find a large number of students' parlors and bed-rooms, the former indicated by Arabic numerals, from 1 to 22, and the latter by the letters *a*, *b*, and *c*, often repeated. The general arrangement is to have one parlor for the common use of the occupants of three lodging-rooms connecting with it. These, you will perceive, are situated along the whole outward side of the building, from the center into the wings, and end at the Professors' houses (T T), in the extremity of each wing. The latter occupy those portions of the building from the first to the fourth story. The total number of students' parlors is one hundred, and of bed-rooms, two hundred and forty-two.

Passing into the eastern part of the center building, we come to the servants' dining hall (M), at the end of which, and separated from it by a small corridor, are the Steward's apartments (I), the Kitchen (L), and Store-room (K). Adjoining the sides of the Hall may be found the Laundry (N), Mangle (O), Laundresses' Office (Q), Drying-room (S), Ironing-rooms (R), and Servants' Bed-rooms (P). The Kitchen and Laundry are perfectly equipped with the most recent materials and implements. In the Wash-room is a five horse-power steam engine, for working the washing machines and mangle. Beneath it is the boiler, in which water, that flows to every part of the building, is heated by a coil of iron pipe, three hundred feet in length, filled with steam. In the oven of the bakery, near the boiler, which is nine by twelve feet in size, all the bread and pastry are baked.

Now let us go up to the second story, or principal floor. Here is a vestibule (V) at the main entrance, twelve by thirty feet in area; and opening into the corridor (U), in front of a spacious double stairway and platform, which occupy an area twenty-eight feet in depth and thirty-eight feet in width. Refer to the plan of

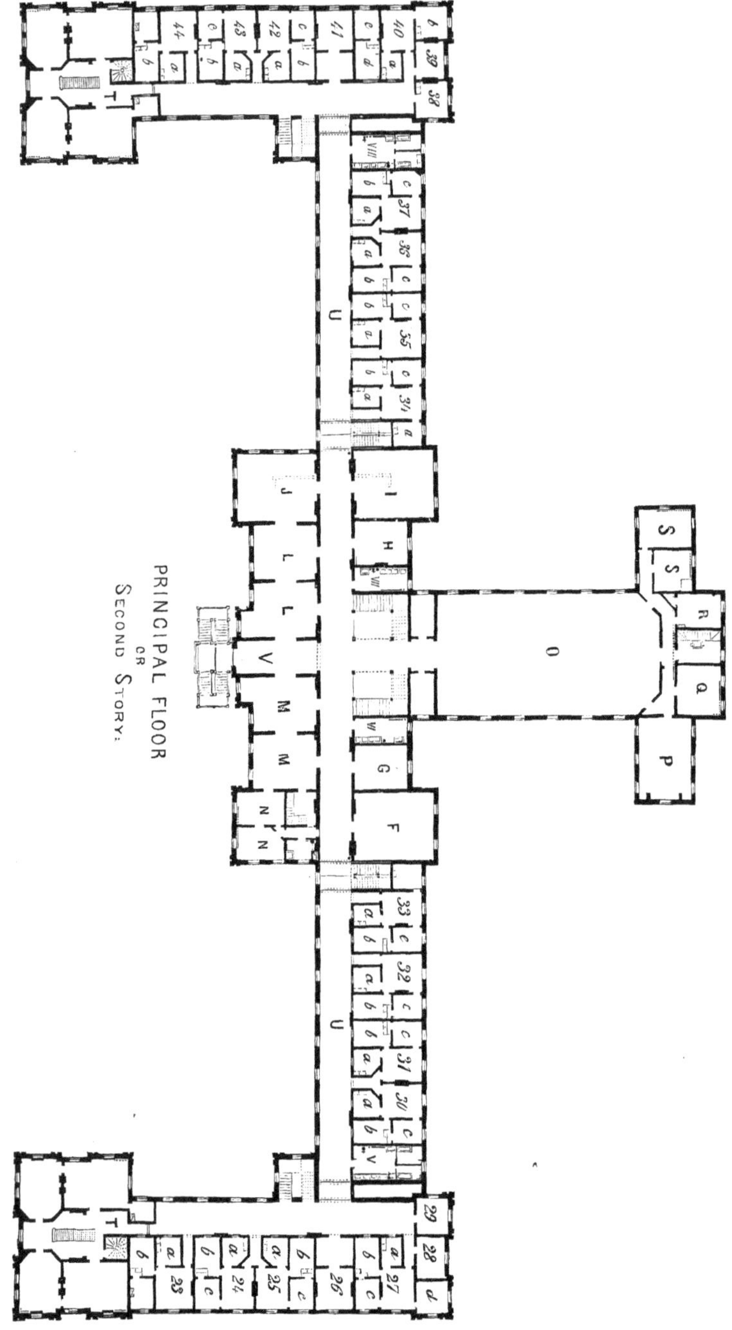
PRINCIPAL FLOOR
OR
SECOND STORY.

this floor on the opposite page as we go along, and you will have a clear idea of its occupation and uses. On both sides of the vestibule are two parlors, each twenty-four by forty-six feet in area, with sliding doors opposite each other. When all of these are thrown back at one

THE CENTRAL DOUBLE STAIRWAY.

time, there is presented an open space twenty-four feet in width, and more than one hundred feet in length. Those on the right of the Vestibule (M, M), are the President's Parlors; and those on the left (L, L) are the College Parlors. The President's house (N, N) adjoins his parlors, and extends from the first to the third story, inclusive.

Adjoining the College Parlors is the Medical Lecture-room (J), which is equipped for instruction with skeletons of both sexes; a manikin, capable of complete dissection; dissectible *papier mâché* models of the eye, ear, and other organs; excellent dried preparations, showing the distribution of nerves and blood-vessels; and a good collection of microscopic objects, to illustrate the minute anatomy of various structures.

Crossing the corridor, we find four Recitation-rooms (I, H, G, F), two on each side of the central stairway. Passing through the door seen in the picture, beneath the landing of the stairway, we enter the great Dining Hall (O), the area of which is forty-five by ninety-four feet. The ceiling, like the rest of this and the next story, is thirteen feet above the floor, and is supported by columns.

On the right of the entrance is the Messenger's room, in which is the only clock in the College, and by which all its prescribed internal movements are directed. In it is also an annunciator, connected with various official apartments, by which right direction is given to answer a summons. In various parts of the building, such as at each end of the four corridors, are electro-magnetic bells, connected with a powerful battery in the Chemical Laboratory. The Messenger has an instrument in her room, by which she can at any moment cause the ringing of one or all of these bells. Governed by the prescriptions of a time table, she announces by a touch of the key of this instrument, causing the bells to ring, the time for rising; for service in the Chapel; for breakfast; for the assembling of classes for instruction, and for the performance of all other prescribed duties at fixed periods of the day.

In the Dining Hall four hundred persons may be seated at table. Back of it is the Carving-room (P), admirably equipped with steam apparatus for keeping every thing for the table warm. Next to it is the Dish-pantry (Q). On the opposite side of a back stairway is the silver and china room (R), with refrigerators in which, and for other purposes, five hundred tons of ice were consumed during

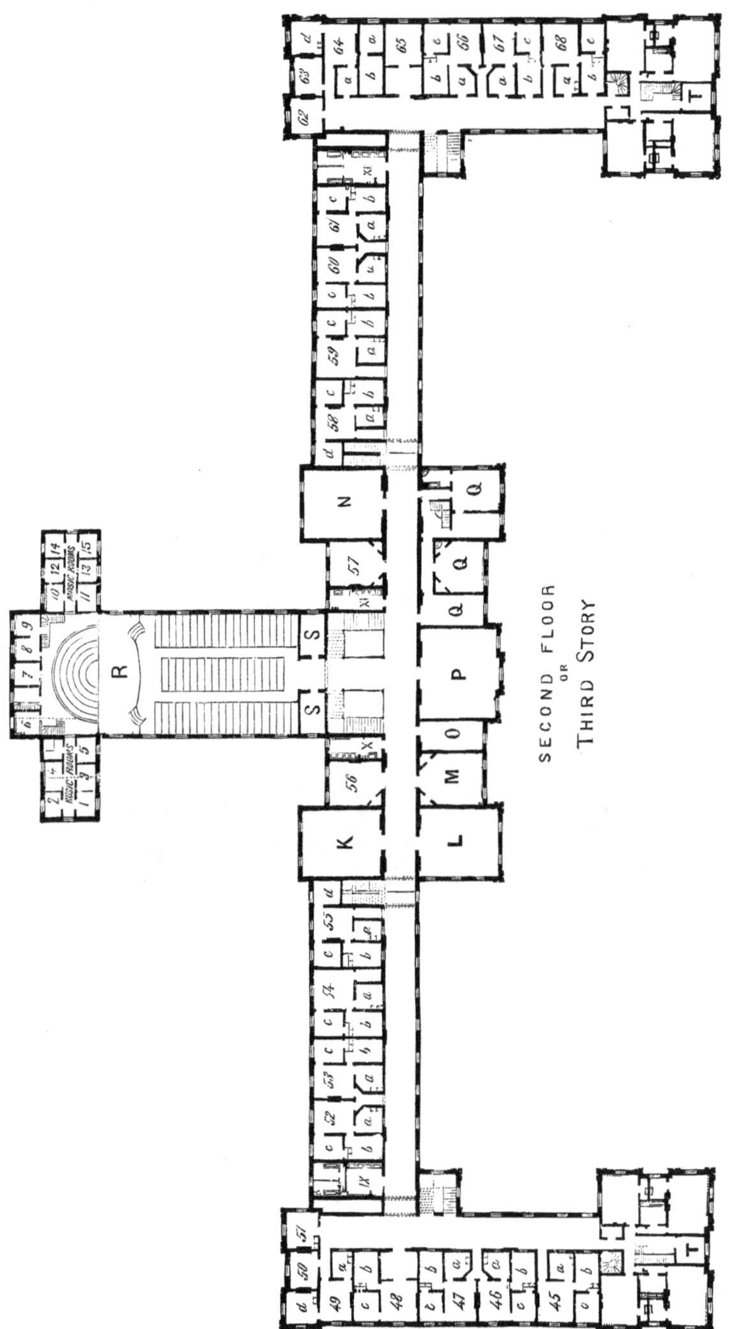
SECOND FLOOR
OR
THIRD STORY
MUSIC ROOMS
MUSIC ROOMS

the first Collegiate year. The rooms S S are for the Steward's use. On this floor, also, are students' parlors and bed-rooms, the former indicated by numerals, from 23 to 44, and the latter by the letters *a*, *b*, and *c*, repeated. T T denote Professors' houses.

We will go up the great stairway to the second floor,

THE CHAPEL, FROM THE GALLERY.

or third story, the plan of which is on the preceding page, and enter the Chapel (R), which is directly over the Dining Hall. It is the same in width as the latter, and is ninety-one feet in length, with a gallery. At its entrance are two cloak-rooms (S S), and at the rear is a semicircular vaulted recess, in which are placed the organ, and seats in gallery form. In front of these is a platform for literary and musical exercises, and exhibitions by the students. The Chapel is neatly furnished, with cushioned seats, and carpeted aisle and platform; and six hundred persons may be comfortably seated in it. Its gallery is supported by brackets below it, and iron rods reaching down from the arched ceiling. At four points of the cornice, as in similar positions in other rooms in the building, the initial of Mr. Vassar's name (V.) is seen inclosed in an arabesque scroll. In the rear of the Chapel, and inclosing the semi-circular recess, are Music-rooms, numbered from 1 to 15.

In front of the Organ, and covering it, is a copy of Raphael's celebrated picture, entitled La Vièrge de Foligno, made with great care by Miss Church, an American woman, who has been for several years in Rome. The original was painted by command of Sigismund Conti of Foligno, who was Secretary to Pope Julius the Second. The story is, that having been, as he supposed, miraculously saved from a thunder-bolt, Sigismund vowed to consecrate a picture upon the altar of the Virgin Mary, to whose protecting care he attributed his salvation. In the upper part of the picture is seen the Virgin in glory, holding the infant Jesus, and surrounded by clouds and angels. On the earth, in the foreground, is a portrait of Sigismund, who is introduced to the Virgin by Jerome, arrayed in the dress of a Cardinal. A figure in the attitude of prayer is intended for St. Francis, near whom stands St. John the Baptist, who points to the Virgin. In the center is a little boy with wings, holding a tablet, on which might be properly inscribed the words of St. Paul to the Athenians—"I perceive that in all things ye are too superstitious." This is one of the most celebrated of Raphael's compositions, and an engraving of it forms the first illustration in the Musée Royale. The donor put it in a church in Rome, from which it was afterward conveyed by his niece, Anna Conti, to the Chapel of the Nunnery of St. Anna, at Foligno, founded by the Conti family. It was among the pictures sent to Paris when Napoleon the First despoiled Italy of its works of art. In 1815 it was sent back to Rome, and placed in the gallery of the Vatican, where Miss Church copied it. That copy, ordered by President Jewett when he was in Rome, in 1861, has been placed temporarily in the Chapel of Vassar College.

On one side of the central stairway, on the floor we are now exploring, is the room of the Lady Principal (56), and on the other side, the apartment of the Matron (57). In the same relative position as on the floors below we find the students' parlors and bed-rooms, the former numbering from 44 to 68, and the latter indicated by the three letters *a*, *b*, and *c*. The Professors' houses are also indicated by the letter T. Directly opposite the Chapel is the Library (P), thirty by thirty-five feet in area, and containing at the present time a little over three thousand volumes. To these large additions will be made, until this portion of the working implements of the College shall be as perfect as any other.

Adjoining the Library, on one side, is the Lady Principal's office (O), and next to it is her parlor. On the other side are the President's apartments (Q Q Q), and across the corridor, opposite, is his office (N). Adjoining the Lady Principal's Parlor is the Cabinet of Natural History (L), and on the opposite side of the corridor is a Recitation-room (K). The former, under the superintendence of the Professor of Natural History, has become one of the most interesting apartments in the College. It contains a large and rapidly increasing collection, among which are now several thousand specimens illustrating mammals, birds, reptiles, fishes, insects, crustacea, shells, echinoderms, acalephs, corals, and sea-anemones. This Cabinet has been enriched, while these pages have been in preparation, by the enlightened generosity of J. P. Giraud, of Poughkeepsie, an amateur Ornithologist, who has presented his entire collection of North American birds to Vassar College, together with rare and valuable works on Ornithology. This collection of birds of North America is said to be equal to any in the world. It contains many specimens of which Audubon made drawings for his magnificent work entitled "Birds of America." Among these is the Great Auk, an aquatic bird now supposed to be extinct. Vassar College will doubtless soon possess the most extensive and valuable museum of Natural History in the country.

Let us now go still higher, to the Third Floor, or Fourth Story. Turning as before at the platform, we enter the gallery of the Chapel (R), at the end of which are music-rooms, numbering from 16 to 31. At the entrance to the gallery are two cloak-rooms (S S); and on each side of the great stairway is a recitation-room (O and P). Extending along the corridor each way, we see students' parlors, numbering from 69 to 95, with bedrooms *a*, *b*, and *c*. At the southeastern angle of this floor are the Physician's room (U), the Infirmary (Q), and Convalescents' room (V). These are delightfully situated, more than fifty feet from the ground, and over-

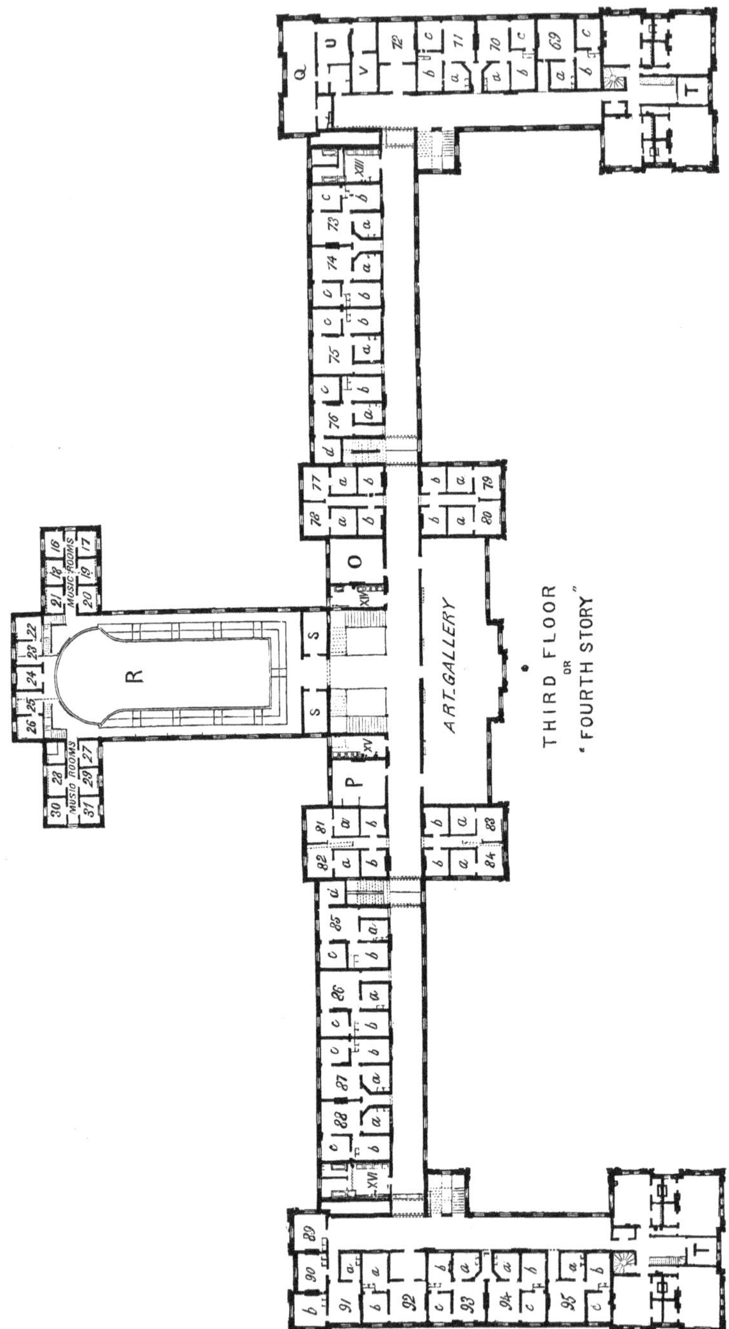
THIRD FLOOR
OR
"FOURTH STORY"
ART GALLERY
MUSIC ROOMS
MUSIC ROOMS
R
S
S
O
P
Q
U
V
T
T

look the most pleasing rural scenery. The view on the east is terminated by high cultivated hills, and on the south by the blue line of the Fish Kil mountains, twenty miles distant. These rooms are well lighted and ventilated, and present in their internal aspect, and scenes from the windows, much to please the eye and cheer the spirits of an invalid. On this floor, also, the Professors' houses are indicated by the letters T T.

Opposite the gallery of the Chapel is the entrance

THE ART GALLERY.

to the Art Gallery. This admits us to a room thirty feet in width and ninety-six feet in length, lighted from a dome in the center that rises about forty feet above the floor, a sky-light in each wing, and windows along the western front of the College. In a greater portion of the apartment, the walls, from the floor well up toward the cornice, are hung with pictures, all adapted by their size and character to the purposes of instruction. This room is in charge of the Professor of Drawing and Painting.

The first prominent object that meets the eye on entering this fine gallery is a full-length portrait of the Founder, painted by Charles Elliott, by order of the Trustees. Immediately below and in front of the portrait may be seen a marble bust of the Founder, life size, by Mrs. Laura S. Hofmann, of Poughkeepsie, who formed the model from life, while the early pages of this Memoir were passing

MATTHEW VASSAR.

through the press. On the walls on each side of the portrait are groups of ancient armor, of much historical interest. That helmet covered with foiled gold came from Spain; and the other, crested by a bird, surmounted the tomb of a family in England, now extinct. That halberd belonged to the French King Francis the First, and his arms are etched on the spear-point. Look into this cuirass, and you will see the names of several of

Cromwell's most noted battles. In those, this shield for the breast and back was used. Here are swords, and gauntlets, and spurs, worn by ancient knights; but we may not stop to consider in detail all that we see in this room. As we enter, we observe on our right a large number of oil paintings, and on our left, a greater number made with water-colors and black-lead pencils; and here and there about the room are students copying pictures, under the direction of the Art Professor. Let us sit down and learn the names of the pictures, and of the artists who made them, from this

CATALOGUE OF THE ART GALLERY OF VASSAR COLLEGE.

OIL PAINTINGS.

1 The Wreck Ashore. *H. Bacon.*
2 A Western Hunter. *J. Crawford Thom.*
3 Landscape. *W. H. Oddie.*
4 The Upper Meadows, North Conway. *Hubbard.*
5 "Behold the Man."
6 A Lesson for the Lazy. *W. H. Beard.*
7 Meadows and Mountains at Bethel. *S. W. Griggs.*
8 The Duck Shooter. *W. Ranney.*
9 Sunset at Lancaster, N. H. *A. D. Shattuck.*
10 Ticonderoga in Winter. *T. L. Smith.*
11 Sunrise on the Bernese Alps. *S. R. Gifford.*
12 Nantasket Beach. *W. H. Gay.*
13 Don Quixote's Attack on the Windmills. *J. Crawford Thom.*
14 Assumption of the Virgin.
15 Summer in South America. *F. E. Church.*
16 Afternoon near Lake George. *J. W. Casilear.*
17 Chocorua Lake and Mountain. *A. D. Shattuck.*
18 Morning over New York. *C. H. Moore.*
19 Glamis Castle. *William Hart.*
20 Dessert Delicacies. *R. Collins.*
21 Interior of St. Germain des Près, Paris. *Duval.*
22 Caught in the Act. *T. H. Matteson.*
23 M. Angelo and his Master-pieces. *J. W. Ehninger.*
24 Through the Woods. *A. B. Durand.*
25 "Where the streamlet sings in rural joy." *A. B. Durand.*
26 Down the Hudson to West Point. *C. H. Moore.*
27 The Culprit Fay. *George Boughton.*
28 Turkish Interior. *Diaz.*
29 The Baron's Tomb. *Müller.*
30 Sacred Song. *Louis Lang.*
31 Evening at Pæstum. *J. F. Cropsey.*
32 The Wild New England Shore. *William Hart.*
33 The Wreath of Nature. *W. F. Richards.*
34 Nature's Nook. *James Hart.*
35 Home again from a Foreign Shore. *Gignoux.*
36 Berkley Rock at Newport. *J. F. Kensett.*
37 Autumn in North America. *F. E. Church.*
38 Birds in the Bushes. *A. F. Tait.*
39 Tuckerman's Ravine. *S. Colman.*
40 Morning on the Coast of Sicily. *J. F. Cropsey.*
41 Evening in Vermont. *F. E. Church.*
42 Robinson praying for the Pilgrims about to embark for Holland. *Edwin White.*
43 Ripley Falls. *B. Champney.*
44 Cellini in his Studio. *Andrier.*
45 Deer in a Dell. *A. F. Tait.*
46 View from Lead Mine Bridge. *William Hart.*
47 The Old Elm by the River Side. *A. J. Bellows.*
48 Sunset in Italy, with Vesper Procession. *D. Johnson.*
49 "Roslyn"—Bryant's Residence. *T. Addison Richards.*
50 "Sunnyside"—Irving's Home. *T. Addison Richards.*
51 Sketch of Madonna and Child. *Rembrandt Lockwood.*
52 The Irish Shepherd. *George Moreland.*
53 The Miser. *Rembrandt Lockwood.*
54 Group from the Village Festival. *Sir David Wilkie.*
55 Near Swallow's Cave, Nahant. *S. W. Griggs.*
56 Chief Justice Marshall. *B. Martin.*

57 Thetis bringing Armor to Achilles. *Benjamin West.*
58 Rainy Day near West Point. *George Broughton.*
59 Interior of a Barn. *Marcus Waterman.*
60 Afternoon on the Androscoggin. *Henry A. Ferguson.*
61 The Upper Connecticut. *A. D. Shattuck.*
62 Crystal Cascade. *Homer Martin.*
63 Cherry Mountain and Franconia Range. *S. L. Gerry.*
64 Glen Ellis Fall. *Homer Martin.*
65 The Lover of Pictures. *J. Crawford Thom.*
66 Autumnal Eve at Valombrosa. *Thomas Cole.*
67 Count Ugolino and Family in the Dungeon of Starvation. *Alonzo Chappel.*
68 Mts. Madison and Adams, from Milan *Alexander Wüst.*
69 The Upper Palisade. *C. H. Moore.*
70 The Visitation (Luke i. 39–56). After *Raphael* and *Del Piombo.*
71 Amiens Cathedral. *Gennisson.*
72 Edward Everett. *J. H. Young.*
73 Lake Winnipiseogee. *Alexander Wüst.*
74 The Catskills in Spring. *C. H. Moore.*
75 Meditation. *R. W. Weir.*
76 Don Quixote in his Study. *F. M. Johnson.*
77 The White Mountains, from Shelburne. *S. L. Gerry.*
78 Sunset on Mole Mountain. *A. D. Shattuck.*
79 Autumnal Snow on Mount Washington. *A. D. Shattuck.*
80 Winter lingering in the Lap of Spring. *B. Champney.*
81 The Saco at North Conway, and Mt. Kearsarge. *William Hart.*
82 The Upper Hudson. *Thomas Doughty.*
83 A Winter View from Newburgh. *L. R. Mignot.*
84 Scenery in Savoy. *Watelet.*
85 Washington at Mt. Vernon. *Alonzo Chappel.*
86 Death of Copernicus. *G. H. Hall.*
87 Exceeding Rich and Precious Promises. *G. H. Hall.*
88 Meadows and Wild Flowers at Conway. *S. Colman.*
89 Dolly Neglected. *W. J. Hennessy.*
90 The Young Devotee. *L'Enfant de Metz.*
91 Tit for Tat. *Duverger.*
92 The Summer Rose. *G. A. Baker.*
93 The Adventure. *W. S. Mount.*
94 Falstaff. *C. L. Elliott.*
95 The Sybil. *D. Huntington.*
96 "The moonshine stealing o'er the scene
Hath blended with the light of eve;
And she was there, my hope, my joy,
My own dear Genevieve." *J. F. Cropsey.*
97 Dead Christ. *M. Alophe.*
98 Beggar Girl in Rome. *Edwin White.*
99 Night over New York. *Alexander Wüst.*
100 Lesson of Prayer. *Henry Peters Gray.*
101 Market Scene in New York. *R. Gignoux.*
102 Noon in Midsummer. *J. McEntee.*
103 The Coming Snow. *J. McEntee.*
104 Artist Brook, North Conway. *S. Colman.*
105 The Shrine of Shakspeare. *S. R. Gifford.*
106 Old Guard. *Mrs. Lily Spencer.*
107 Warwick Castle and River Avon. *E. W. Nichols.*
108 Sybil. After *Domenichino.*
109 Spring at Great Barrington. *H. A. Ferguson.*
110 Summer in North Conway. *H. A. Ferguson.*
111 Autumn at Lake George. *H. A. Ferguson.*
112 Winter near Albany. *H. A. Ferguson.*
113 Lamentation over Jerusalem. *Begas.*
114 The Spanish Devotee. *Greene.*
115 The Jewess. *E. Dodge.*
116 Narraganset Coast. *Marcus Waterman.*
117 Flower Girl at the Church Door. *Achenbach.*
118 The Old Man's Lesson. *Thomas Hicks.*
119 Talk Beach, near Cohasset. *W. Gay.*
120 Lake Maggiore. *S. R. Gifford.*
121 Old Cottage near Shakspeare's Birth-place. *J. M. Falconer.*
122 The Roman Campagna. *S. R. Gifford.*
123 Sunset at Bethel, Maine. *A. D. Shattuck.*
124 Down the Willey Pass. *S. Colman.*
125 The Franconia Notch, and Mt. Lafayette. *A. J. Bellows.*
126 Sunset in Western Virginia. *W. L. Sontag.*
127 The American Monk. *Rembrandt Lockwood.*
128 Noon near the Lake. *George Inness.*
129 Summer Twilight on the Catskills. *Jamieson.*
130 Cape Blow-me-down, Canada. *Le Grand.*
131 Evening in the Meadows. *George Inness.*
132 Head of the River. *Alexander Wüst.*
133 Evening on the Mystic. *J. Henry Hill.*

PICTURES IN WATER COLOR, AND PENCIL DRAWINGS.

134 On the Seine. *Ghirardi.*
135 The Upper Rhine. *Louis Thomas.*
136 French Cavalry. *Thos. Fort.*
137 The Diligence. *Thos. Fort.*
138 Bridge over the Rhone. *Bethune.*
139 La Grandmère.
140 York Cathedral. *W. Richardson.*
141 Flamboyant Church. *Croydon.*
142 Manor House, York. *Richardson.*
143 The Truant. *Taylor.*
144 The Observatory, Oxford. *William Westall.*
145 Trinity Library, Cambridge. *Westall.*
146 Jesus College, Cambridge. *Westall.*
147 Marine. *Unknown.*
148 Kitchen, Christ Ch. College, Oxford. *A. Pugin.*
149 Chapel of Magdalen College, Cambridge. *Pugin.*
150 Caius College, Cambridge. *Pugin.*
151 The Sinner and The Saviour. *West.*
152 Crypt of St. Peter's, Oxford. *F. Mackenzie.*
153 Court of Emanuel College, Cambridge. *Pugin.*
154 St. Peter's College, Cambridge. *W. Westall.*
155 Emanuel College, Cambridge. *W. Westall.*
156 St. Paul's School, London. *Mackenzie.*
157 Caius College, Cambridge. *Pugin.*
158 Chapel of Emanuel College, Cambridge. *Pugin.*
159 Worcester College, Oxford. *John H. Le Keux.*

160 Dining Hall, King's College, Cambridge. *Pugin.*
161 Chapel of Clare Hall, Cambridge. *Mackenzie.*
162 Wradesbury Mill. *Le Keux.*
163 St. John's College, Oxford. *Pugin.*
164 Library and Senate House, Cambridge. *Mackenzie.*
165 Buildwey Abbey. *E. Dayes.*
166 St. John's Tower, Chester. *Le Keux.*
167 Pen-and-ink Sketch. *Col. John Trumbull.*
168 East End of Winchester Cathedral. *Mackenzie.*
169 Salisbury Cross. *Girtin* and *Turner.*
170 Conway. *H. Pyne.*
171 Door to Cloisters, York. *Richardson.*
172 Evening, and Becalmed Ship. *W. C. Knell.*
173 From Poets' Corner, Westminster Abbey. *John Nash.*
174 Norman Door, St. Peter's, Oxford. *F. Alexander.*
175 A Persian Ruin. *Dibdin.*
176 Egyptian Dancing Girls. *P. C. French.*
177 Afloat. *Knell.*
178 French Peasants at a Fountain. *Teichet.*
179 Bangor Abbey, North Wales. *J. Webber.*
180 Norman Church. *E. Clay.*
181 Chapel of Jesus College, Cambridge. *Pugin.*
182 Hall of Harstmonceau. *S. S. Dod.*
183 The Wreck. *Knell.*
184 Eagle Tower, Carnarvon Castle. *Le Keux.*
185 Haddon Hall. *J. Lewis.*
186 The Scholar and Soldier. *George Cattermole.*
187 Tivoli, Italy. *W. H. Burnett.*
188 Old House, York. *Richardson.*
189 Six English Cathedrals. *Austin* and *Williams.*
190 Thatched Cottage in France. *A. O.*
191 Scene from Sheridan. *Wright.*
192 The Ghost Story. *Alonzo Chappel.*
193 Sketch in Spain. *David Roberts.*
194 Beaver Brook, White Mountains. *Homer Martin.*
195 Round Tower in Sussex. *Samuel Prout.*
196 Kitchen, Netley Abbey. *H. Pyne.*
197 Playing Marbles. *Lysor.*
198 Twilight on the Upper Seine. *Madame Michelet.*
199 Apple Tree Branch. *Pauline Allain.*
200 Rheinstein, on the Rhine. *Le Keux.*
201 Chapel of Henry the Seventh. *John Nash.*
202 Sabrina Disenchanted. *Richard Westall.*
203 Westminster Hall. *John Nash.*
204 A Spanish Ruin. *Le Saint.*
205 Wife of Andrea del Sarto.
206 Salisbury Plain, with Stonehenge. *Le Keux.*
207 The Vesper Bell. *Barrett.*
208 The Sacristan. *John Gilbert.*
209 Marine View. *Chambers.*
210 Ruins in Auvergne France. *J. D. Harding.*
211 Coronation of Cnarles VII., in Rheims Cathedral. *J. E. Buckley.*
212 Morning on the Lower Thames. *Melville.*
213 The Offering. *Coke Smyth.*
214 Coningsbury Park. *Pyne.*
215 Haddon Hall. *Harding.*
216 Interior of Salisbury Cathedral. *Mackenzie.*
217 Italian Ruins. *Earp.*
218 Lady Chapel, Salisbury Cathedral. *Cattermole.*
219 Landscape View in France. After *Turner.*
220 Old World Homes. *C. Mozin.*
221 Market House near Windsor Castle. *Thomas Allon.*
222 Morning on the Thames. *J. Varley.*
223 Blue-Eyed Mary. *Bourier.*
224 Dust Ho! *Gavarni.*
225 Fight for the Prey. *Nestfield.*
226 Cheddar Cliffs. *J. Jackson.*
227 Ruined Abbey. *Hoffman.*
228 Ripon Cathedral. *Le Keux.*
229 River of Romance. *Jules Nefo.*
230 The Beacon Church. *Clarkson Stanfield.*
231 The Monk amid Ruins. *Fleury.*
232 Norman Tower and Terrace. *Hubert.*
233 Upton Church, near Windsor Castle. *Le Keux.*
234 Juliet and Nurse. *Henry Warren.*
235 The Four Elements. *Henry Corbould.*
236 Spring, Woods, and Wild Flowers. *Davidson.*
237 Two Gentlemen of Verona. *Wright.*
238 Take Care! *Haverhie.*
239 Cassonburg. *William Hunt.*
240 Soane's Museum, London. *Penry Williams.*
241 Hay Harvest. *J. H. Mole.*
242 Wayside Chapel in Normandy. *G. Hess.*
243 Sketch on the Medway. *Stanfield.*
244 Oriental Lady. *John Lewis.*
245 Original Chalk Study. *Sir David Wilkie.*
246 Monastery of St. John at Ephesus. *Brokenden.*
247 Coast of Arran, Scotland. *Houston.*
248 Jealousy. *Beaume.*
249 Greek Brigands. *Sir Charles Eastlake.*
250 Interior of York Castle. *W. H. Bartlett.*
251 View of Salisbury. *Bartlett* and *Pyne.*
252 Crossing the Brook. *Beaubeuff.*
253 River Side in France. *Anastasi.*
254 View of Norwood. *Pyne.*
255 Decline of Day in Italy. *Charles Vacher.*
256 Regent's Park, London. *Bartlett.*
257 Celtic Monuments in France. *Bourgeois.*
258 Church at Harfleur, on the Seine. *Marson.*
259 Ely Cathedral. *Clennell.*
260 Twilight. *J. Salmon.*
261 Sunset. *J. Salmon.*
262 Noon. *J. Salmon.*
263 Forenoon. *J. Salmon.*
264 Morning. *J. Salmon.*
265 St. Peter's at Caen, Normandy. *Charles Vacher.*
266 Nevill's Court, Trinity College, Cambridge. *Buckler.*
267 Scene in Holland. *Neusen.*
268 St. Peter's and the Vatican, Rome. *Amici.*
269 Ruined Castle. *Dewint.*
270 Summer Shower *Mapleston.*
271 Old Houses in Bristol. *Hardwick.*
272 Adoration of Shepherds.
273 The Pantheon, Rome. *Amici.*
274 Church at Rouen. *H. Jenkens.*
275 St. Mark's, Venice. *Samuel Prout.*
276 Venice, seen from the Grand Canal. *William Wyld.*
277 The Open Sea. *J. Salmon.*

278 Hall at Knowle, Kent. *J. Nash.*
279 Holy Family. *John Absolon.*
280 Aspiration. *Gavarni.*
281 Old Greenwich. *J. Salmon.*
282 Norman Tower and Mill, Oxford. *Le Keux.*
283 Eton College. *Le Keux.*
284 Chivalry. *Louis David.*
285 Classic Ruin by Moonlight. *F. O. Finch.*
286 Nestley Abbey by Torchlight. *J. E. Buckley.*
287 Fortitude. *Eugene Delacroix.*
288 Deer in Devonshire Park. *C. Pearson.*
289 Sea Shore and Monastic Ruins. *Salmon.*
290 Sterling Castle, and the field of Bannockburn. *Houston.*
91 The Church at Stoke, near Windsor. *Croydon.*
92 Berne, Switzerland. *J. M. W. Turner.*
93 Bacharach, on the Rhine. *Turner.*
94 Pass of St. Bernard. *Turner.*
95 Sandy Knowe and Smailholm Tower. *Turner.*
96 Tomb of Henry III., Westminster Abbey. *Scandrett.*
97 Reading the Legend. *Karl Hartmann.*
98 Cadir Iris and Snowdon, North Wales. *Copley Fielding.*
99 Ruined Castle above Baden-Baden. *Wyld.*
00 Cæsar's Tower, Essex. *George Tripp.*
01 Interior of St. Mark's, Venice. *Lake Price.*
02 Sketch of Church and Bay at Naples. *John Ruskin.*
03 Lucerne, Switzerland. *T. Richardson.*
04 Tower Hill, London. *Le Keux.*
05 Bay Window. *Prout.*
06 St. Stephen's Church, London. *Pugin.*
07 Coronation of William IV., in Westminster Abbey. *David Roberts.*
08 Christmas. *John Martin.*
09 Joan of Arc in Prison at Rouen. *J. E. Buckley.*
0 The End. *Herring.*
1 Ducks and Flowers. *Wiegal.*
2 Game Fowls. *Wiegal.*
3 Italian Landscape. *Leitch.*
4 Loch Katrine. *Rowbotham.*
5 The Village Aristocrat. *Tigal.*
6 St. Martin dividing his Cloak with the Beggars. After *Rubens* and *Vandyke*, by *West.*
7 Saumur, on the Loire. *Eugene Soulez.*
8 Exeter Cathedral. *J. Buckler.*
9 An Old Buck and Companion. *T. S. Cooper.*
0 Merton College, Oxford. *N. A. Delamotte.*
1 St. Mary's Abbey, York. *Richardson.*
2 King's College, Cambridge. *Mackenzie.*
3 Therborne, Dorset. *Le Keux.*
4 Exeter College, Oxford. *Delamotte.*
5 Belenzona, Italy. *J. Eden.*
6 Melrose Cross. *Turner.*
7 Interior of Oxford Cathedral. *Delamotte.*
8 Kenilworth Castle. *Archer.*
9 Depedene Park, Surry. *Bartlett.*
Crypt of Holy Trinity, Caen. *J. S. Cotman.*
Merton Library, Oxford. *Delamotte.*
George IV. Dining his Court in the Chinese Pavilion at Brighton.

333 Botanic Garden, Oxford. *Delamotte.*
334 St. John's College, Oxford. *Delamotte.*
335 Rouveredo, Italy. *J. Eden.*
336 University Boat Race on the Isis, Oxford. *Delamotte.*
337 Nash's Castle, Isle of Wight. *W. Daniels.*
338 Walraken Church, Norfolk. *Cattermole.*
339 Cloisters at Townloins. *Bagster.*
340 Conway Castle. *Pyne.*
341 Bust of Henry Clay. *Hart.*
342 St. Mary's, Cambridge. *Mackenzie.*
343 Depedene, Surry. *Bartlett.*
344 Library of Merton College, Oxford. *Pugin.*
345 Rugby School. *Pugin.*
346 Winchester School. *Pugin.*
347 Pembroke College, Oxford. *Le Keux.*
348 Cloisters, Eton College. *Pugin.*
349 Dining Hall, Trinity College, Cambridge. *Mackenzie.*
350 St. John's College, Cambridge. *Mackenzie.*
351 Interior of St. Mary's, Cambridge. *Mackenzie.*
352 Westminster School. *Pugin.*
353 Baliol College Chapel, Oxford. *Le Keux.*
354 Canons Ashby. *G. Shepherd.*
355 Cloister of Chester Cathedral. *Le Keux.*
356 Twilight on Lake and Ruin. *Robertson.*
357 St. Paul's, London. *Thompson.*
358 Chepstow Castle. *Webber.*
359 Druidical Remains. *Bartlett.*
360 Bust of Daniel Webster. *Clevanger.*
361 Corsham House. *Prout* and *Repton.*
362 Trafalgar Monument, London. *J. R. Thompson.*
363 Winchester Cathedral. *Mackenzie.*
364 Sir Walter Scott's Monument. *Chercher.*
365 Capitals in Salisbury Cathedral. *Mackenzie.*
366 Norman Church Architecture. *Louis Thomas.*
367 Norman Domestic Architecture. *Louis Thomas.*
368 Abbey on the Loire. *Gobeaud.*
369 Battle of Marengo. *Fosbry.*
370 French Landscape. *Gobeaud.*
371 The Model Asleep. *Millais.*
372 Head of Maclise. *Hennesay.*
373 White Mountain Range from Jefferson Hill. *William Hart.*
374 Moonlight on Mount Carter, Gorham. *Hart.*
375 Cartoon for a Votive Picture. *Victor Orsel.*
376 Winged Head. *Orsel.*
377 Peace. *William Etty*
378 War. *Etty.*
379 View down the Androscoggin, from Milan Bridge. *Hart.*
380 Lower Berlin Falls. *Hart.*
381 White Mountains from Shelburne. *Hart.*
382 View from Milan, above the Bridge. *Hart.*
383 Turner's Autograph.
384 Death of Abel.
385 The Battle of the Amazons. Bronze.
386 Ancient Arms and Armor.
387 Welsh Women returning from Market. *David Cox.*

COPIES.

388 St. Peter's and the Vatican.
389 The Pantheon at Rome.
390 Niagara.
391 Cologne from the Rhine.
392 Edge of the Wood.
393 English Landscape. After *Müller.*
394 The Mountain Stream.
395 Eton College. After *Ludlow.*
396 Court of Eton College. *The same.*
397 Windsor Castle from the Great Park. After *Pyne.*
398 Windsor Castle. *The same.*
399 Sappho.
400 St. Peter's and Vatican. *Photograph.*
401 The Colosseum, Rome. *Photograph.*
402 The Roman Forum. *Photograph.*
403 Fine Line Engraving of Oxford. After *Turner.*
404 The Good and the Bad. After *Orsel.*
405 Glasgow Cathedral. After *David Roberts.*
406 Interior of Milan Cathedral. After *Prout.*
407 Exterior of Milan Cathedral. *The same.*
408 Midnight Mass. After *Haghe.*
409 View from St. Elmo Castle, Naples.
410 Interior of the Tribune, Florence.
411 Salisbury Cathedral.
412 Durham Cathedral.
413 The Meeting of Raphael and Michael Angelo. After *Horace Vernet.*
414 Winchester Cathedral.
415 Incredulity of St. Thomas. Copied by *Miss Church* from *Guercino.*
416 The Blessed Mother. After *Dolce.* by *the same.*
417 La Vièrge de Foligno.
418 Ancient Stained Glass.
419 Bust of Scott.
420 Bust of Byron.
421 Bust of Milton.
422 Bust of Shakspeare.

This catalogue reveals, in a degree, the treasures of the Art Gallery of Vassar College. These may only be estimated after considering the further record, that the pictures are accompanied by almost a thousand volumes illustrative of the Fine Arts, some of them the most rare and valuable ever published. Scattered through this library, in bound folios, are thousands of original water-color sketches, pencil drawings, and engravings, from the hands of some of the most eminent modern artists. The collection is particularly rich in architectural drawings, especially such as illustrate ecclesiology, in all its forms of church and cathedral structure and decoration, in Great Britain and on the Continent. A large portion of these drawings are from the immense treasure of this kind that belonged to the late venerable antiquary, and author of more than eighty illustrated works, John Britton, who permitted the collector of the books and pictures in the Art Gallery of Vassar College to draw from them without stint. John Le Keux, many of whose works are in this collection, led him to rich stores; and other friends abroad, like Samuel Rogers, the poet, Sir

Charles Barry, John Ruskin, Baring Brothers, and others, kindly gave him their efficient assistance.

The collection of water-color pictures is, without doubt, superior to any other in this country. In a note to the author of this Memoir, the collector says: "Almost every great hand that built the finest school of water-color on earth is represented in the Vassar College collection; many of the present age by works ordered for it." Among these water-color pictures are four sketches by Turner, one of which has a peculiar value, because it contains the work of three eminent contemporary artists on one small piece of paper. It is a sketch of the Pass of St. Bernard (294), which is engraved in Rogers's *Italy*. The landscape is by Turner; a dead body in the snow is by Charles Stothard; and the two dogs, which appear a little outside of the picture, are from pencil sketches by Sir Edwin Landseer.

It would be a delight to go through this library and about the gallery, and examine in detail the most celebrated of the works before us. But this we may not do, and we must be contented with stopping a few minutes to enjoy the most remarkable. Among the "elephant folios," elegantly bound, we find the Musée Royale and the Musée Française; engravings and descriptions of the pictures, statues, bas-reliefs, and cameos in the gallery of the Pitti Palace, in Florence; illuminated books of the middle ages; Carter's Ancient Sculpture and Painting in England; Coltman's Architectural Antiquities of Normandy; Britton's Exeter Cathedral, in which are bound up the original drawings by Wyatt, from which all the engravings of the work were made; Knight's Ecclesiastical Architecture of Italy; Royal Gallery of British Art; Gallery of Vienna; Gallery of the Duke of Orleans, and many others of great value and rarity.

Among the works of art is a perfect copy, by the electrotype process, of the celebrated silver dish now in possession of the King of Prussia, on which is delineated,

Battle of the Amazons.

by a wonderful grouping of figures in low relief, the story of the Battle of the Amazons, which employed the genius of Rubens and other masters. The early history of this dish is unknown. More than twenty years ago, it was found in the hands of an antiquary in Cologne, and was purchased by the Prussian monarch for about twelve thousand dollars. It bears internal evidence of having been made full three hundred years ago, by Benvenuto Cellini, who was a favorite of Cosmo de Medici, the Grand Duke of Tuscany, and ranks high as a sculptor, and as the greatest medalist the world has ever seen. None but an artist possessed of his genius could have wrought the dish whose ornamentation is given in outline in the sketch on the foregoing page.

That story of the Battle of the Amazons is found among the most ancient of the classic fictions. It represents a community or nation of women, athletic, fully developed, and warlike, giving offensive or defensive battle to men whenever occasion required. Like all others of those old fictions, it was intended to illustrate some physical or moral power, and, like them, it has greatly taxed the ingenuity of antiquaries to explain its hidden meaning. None believe it to be an historical fact. Some suppose it to represent the conquest of one form of religion over another, and especially the spread of the worship of the Ephesian Diana over the then known world; while others believe that it personated the right of woman to contend for equality with man, and typified her final victory. We will accept the latter interpretation, and regard the great metal plate hanging in its Art Gallery as the typical shield of Vassar College, the first fully armed champion of the right of woman to all the knowledge that man may possess.

Among the pictures around us are many whose history is exceedingly interesting. If you wish to learn it, look into that black-covered Manuscript Catalogue lying there, prepared by the collector of the pictures and books.

Who is he? you may inquire. He is the Reverend Elias L. Magoon, D. D., a clergyman in Albany, New York, of the Baptist denomination, and one of the Trustees of this College. For nearly a dozen years he was assiduous at home and abroad, as means and opportunity offered, in making this collection. When the gallery was finished, the proper committee wondered how they should cover its bare walls with appropriate implements of education in art. Their desires were more than satisfied when the generous Founder gave Dr. Magoon twenty thousand dollars for his treasures, and presented them to the Trustees of the Institution. Thus munificence, acting in unison with the previous labors of taste, has given to Vassar College the means for instruction in art possessed by no other seminary of learning in this country.

We have lingered long in the Art Gallery; let us now go up to the attic floor, and search for objects of interest there. Around this open court are only baggage-rooms (C); and a little to the westward are students' parlors, numbering from 96 to 100, with two bed-rooms each. At the extremity of the long passage over the Chapel, on the right, are Vocal Music rooms (E E), and on the left are Drawing Studios (D D), where the elements of art are taught, and for which purpose drawings and plaster casts are furnished in abundance. In each of the towers (F F), at the inner angle formed by the center building and the wings, and over this floor, is an immense water-tank, and three others are nearer the center. From them, in a manner that will be mentioned presently, about twenty thousand gallons of pure water are distributed through the building each day. In the extremities of the wings on this floor are the servants' rooms (G G).

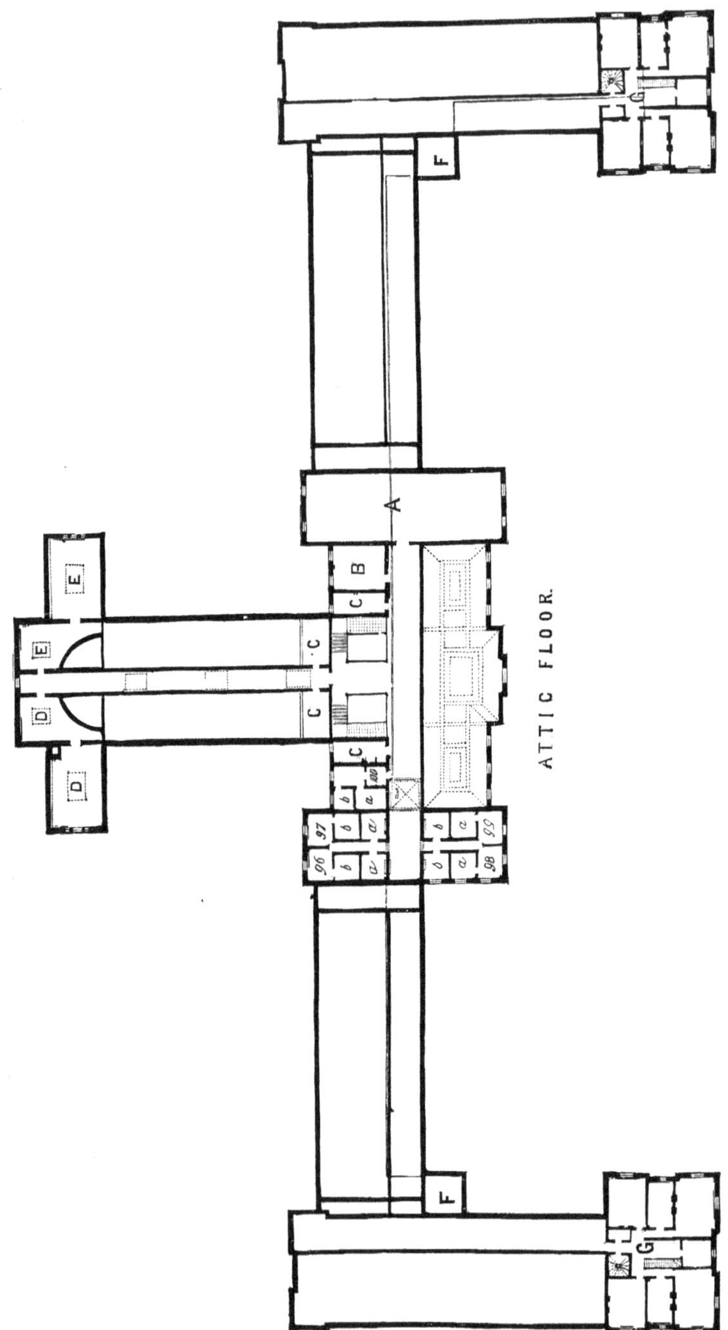
ATTIC FLOOR.
A
B
C
C
C
C
C
D
D
E
E
F
F
G
G
96
97
98
99
100
a
b

Looking around this floor, you would little suspect the treasures of science it contains, in the two rooms marked A and B on the plan. These are the Cabinets of Geology, Mineralogy, and Lithology, and present one of the most complete and best arranged collections of specimens of rocks, minerals, and fossils, in the country. The Lithological Cabinet is nineteen by twenty-one feet in area; that of Geology and Mineralogy is twenty-four by seventy-five feet. The latter is a most attractive place for the general observer as well as the philosopher. The first object that meets the eye as you enter, is the model of an immense fossil Armadillo (*Schisto-pleurum*), found near Buenos Ayres, whose length, including the head and tail, is eight feet six inches, and its height nearly five feet. It is seen in the center of the room in the accompanying picture. The body and tail of the original are at Dijon, in France, and the head is in the Garden of Plants, in Paris. This division of the treasure is the result of a compromise between two claimants to the possession of the whole fossil. The model of the head was procured for Vassar College only one year ago.

The arrangement of the specimens in these cabinets has been made with special reference to instruction. The Cabinet of Mineralogy is so compiled as to first illustrate all the elementary questions of the science, such as relate to the structure, growth, form, and external features of minerals; and thus presents, in a systematic collection, all the well-known and important mineral species which are met with in nature in all parts of the world. The prominent features of this cabinet appear under four sections: the first illustrating Crystallography; the second, the Physical Properties of Minerals; the third, a Working Collection; and the fourth, a Systematic Collection. The first section shows several series of natural and artificial crystals. The second section is divided into nine series: the first giving examples of kinds and degrees of the luster of minerals; the second, their colors and shades of color; the third, their diaphaneity or degree of transmission or interruption of light; the fourth illustrates

Cabinet of Geology and Mineralogy.

the refraction and polarization of light in various minerals; the fifth, their phosphorescence; the sixth, their electrical and magnetical properties; the seventh, their degrees of specific gravity; the eighth, a scale of their hardness; and the ninth, the variety of their taste and odor.

The third, or Working Section, contains about fifteen hundred specimens of minerals, intended for close examination by the students in every variety of experiment. The fourth section, or Systematic Collection, consists of about two thousand specimens, classified according to Dana's system of Mineralogy. It includes about six hundred varieties, represented by several specimens, including the crystallized and amorphous condition. Each specimen is neatly arranged upon a block and labeled. The detached crystals are in part mounted on upright brass holders, the name, form, &c., being inscribed on the pedestal beneath.

The Cabinet of Geology consists of about four thousand specimens of rocks, fossils, &c., arranged in several distinct sections. The first section is a Lithological collection, in which are represented about five hundred specimens of all the known varieties of rocks, arranged in complete illustration of the science of Lithology, and representative of the mineral masses which constitute the crust of our globe. These are arranged in twelve distinct series. The second section is a Paleontological collection, in which are over three hundred specimens of fossils, showing all the important types of animal life, as recorded in "God's elder Scriptures," written on the crust of the earth. These are arranged on blocks of wood and labeled. The fossils of each Geological epoch are carefully grouped with a determinate Zoölogical order, and show the types and species of animal life which characterized each epoch. In this manner, assisted by plaster casts of the larger and rarer fossils, a comprehensive view is given of the features of each period.

For the purpose of further illustrating the whole science of Geology, the Cabinet contains about fifty Geological charts and landscapes, intended to show the succession of strata and the groups of animal and vegetable life in each of the periods. Some of these pictures show the forms of such strange animals, that it is no wonder Lucretius wrote, with excited imagination, after seeing (as we may fairly believe he did) the skeleton of one of them--

> "Hence, doubtless, earth prodigious forms at first
> Gendered, of face and members most grotesque;
> Monsters—half man, half woman—shapes unsound,
> Footless and handless, void of mouths or eye,
> Or, from misjunction, maimed of limb with limb."

This Cabinet is also furnished with models, in relief, of noted volcanoes, and wooden models illustrating the various phenomena of stratification, faults, &c. These cabinets, which so completely illustrate the whole science of Geology, were collected and thus admirably arranged by Professor H. A. Ward, of Rochester, New York, and were purchased of him for Vassar College.

We have now visited every part of the College edifice, from the cellar to the attic; let us see what we may find of interest outside of it.

THE OBSERVATORY.

Yonder, about eight hundred feet northeast of the College building, is the Observatory, already mentioned, standing on the summit of a rocky knoll, at the eastern verge of the Campus of seventy acres. Its foundations are about ten feet above the general level of the plain, which is two hundred feet higher than the Hudson River. Come! we may explore it with a certainty of being well rewarded.

Follow into this crypt-like entrance, and up this narrow stairway. This is the room in which are the Astronomical Clock, and the Chronograph connected with it, for recording observations. How pleasantly we are greeted by this venerable man, the father of the Professor of Astronomy in Vassar College, who first taught her young eyes how to explore the heavens—

"Far as the Solar Walk or Milky Way,"

and her young mind to grasp the idea that startled the poet when he said:—

"How distant some of those nocturnal suns!
So distant, says the sage, 't were not absurd
To doubt, if beams set out at Nature's birth
Are yet arrived at this so foreign world;
Though nothing half so rapid as their flight!"

We are fortunate in having a friend so kind and competent to show us the instruments and explain their uses. With the descriptions given us by Professor Farrar, under whose direction the Observatory was built and equipped, this visit may be made very interesting and instructive. The accompanying diagram, kindly furnished by him, illustrates the meridian section and the ground-plan of the Observatory. The building consists, in altitude, of a basement, principal story, and dome; and in area, of an octagonal center and three wings. In the diagram of the meridian section, A A indicate the terrace; B, the native rock; and C, the surface of the plain. In the ground plan, D indicates a stairway leading up to a flat roof; E, the Transit room; F, the Prime

Vertical room; G, the Clock and Chronograph room; H and K, the Clock and Chronograph piers; M, the Equatorial room; N, an open stone platform, and O, a covered stone platform. The scale is forty-eight feet to an inch. The octagon is twenty-six feet from face to

MERIDIAN SECTION. GROUND PLAN.

face, and is surmounted by a dome twenty-five feet seven inches in extreme diameter. The wings are all of one size and form, being each twenty-one by twenty-eight feet in extreme dimensions, making the entire length of the building eighty-two feet.

The basement of the wings is nine feet in height, but the floor of the octagon (which is of the same external height) is four and a half feet above the corresponding floors of the wings. The vertex of the dome is thirty-eight feet above the foundation. Its form is a hemisphere, upon a cylinder of two feet altitude. All the walls of the building are of brick, and the piers for instruments, of stone. The platforms are made of large flag-stone, and the railings and stairways, of iron. The walls of the octagon are solid, varying in thickness, and afford a cylinder of great stability. Those of the wings are hollow. The dome is constructed of ribs of pine, resting on a circular plate of the same material, and is covered with heavy sheet-tin. Upon another circular wooden plate, bolted to the top of the cylindrical wall, it is made to revolve very easily by an arrangement of sixteen cast-iron pulleys, nine inches in diameter, running on a circular track of iron. Half of them are grooved, and the remainder are only friction rollers. There is a contrivance of wheels and crank, by which a force of only ten pounds is required to move the great dome, that weighs a ton and a half. The opening in the dome for the Equatorial is twenty inches.

The east or Transit wing, and north or Prime Vertical wing, have each a slit in the walls and roof, twenty inches wide, for instrumental observations. The south or Clock and Chronograph wing is furnished with apparatus to keep those instruments in a proper temperature in winter.

There are five stone piers, built up from the native rock to the principal floors, on which the instruments rest. These piers are all disconnected at every point from the walls and floors of the building, so that they are as immovable by wind or any mechanical force as the rock on which they stand. The most massive of these is the Equatorial pier, which tapers upward. The base is eight and a half by nine and a half feet in area, and it is thirteen and a half feet in height. Upon this rests a granite shaft that holds the great instrument. The two shafts for the Transit and Meridian Circle are of Onondaga limestone; those for the Prime Vertical are of white Westchester marble; and the bases of the Clock and Chronograph are mottled Dover marble. The roofs of the wings, on to which the students go for observations, are surrounded by substantial iron railings.

Such is the Observatory building. Now let us look at the instruments, and learn their structure and uses. This Astronomical Clock and the Chronograph connected with it are very perfect instruments, manufactured in the establishment of William Bond & Sons, in Boston. The clock dial warns us not to linger too long here; so pass up the short flight of steps to the floor under the great revolving dome, which the strength of a little child may move. Here is the great Equatorial Refractor, second only, when it was mounted, to three in the United States in the size of its object-glass, which was thoroughly tested and highly approved by Professor Rutherford. The exceptions were the great telescopes at Cambridge, at Hamilton College, and at the Dudley Observatory. This is the last large instrument of the kind made by the late Henry Fitz. The diameter of the object-glass is twelve inches and three-eighths, clear aperture; and its focal length sixteen and a half feet. The hour-circle is eighteen inches in diameter, and reads by verniers to four seconds of time. The declination-circle is twenty inches in diameter, and reads by verniers to thirty seconds of arc. The instrument has nine negative eye-pieces, of powers ranging from fifty to fifteen hundred, for direct observation; also a superior finding telescope, whose object-glass is three inches in diameter. A driving clock, by which the object is kept constantly in the field of view of the telescope, is attached to the mounting. Other valuable appurtenances are a Ring Micrometer, of diameter appropriate to the field of the instrument; a large position Filar Micrometer, provided with eight positive eye-pieces, and so constructed that either the field or the wires may be illuminated at pleasure, and a Spectroscope, for the examination of the various spectra from celestial objects. In the adjoining room, at the east, which is reached by a descent of a few steps, is the Transit and Meridian Circle, with a telescope of such power that it has revealed to the eye of the observer the time-star delta Ursa Minoris, of the fifth magnitude, at ten o'clock in the morning. The

FIRST ASTRONOMICAL OBSERVATION AT VASSAR COLLEGE.

first observation with this instrument made by students of Vassar College, under the directions of Miss Mitchell, was the meridian passage of Aldebaran, on a bright autumnal day, as a part of a class exercise. One of the students knelt, with her eye to the glass, watching the star as it passed behind the threads in the focus of the instrument, while her companion noted the time by a chronometer on which she was looking, when the star seemed to touch those threads. So interesting was the scene, that a few weeks later, when a photographer was at the

College, a sun-picture of the two pupils and the instrument, in the same position, was made at the request of the Professor of Astronomy.

The Transit and Meridian Circle is of the same size, pattern, and adjustments as that made by the same manufacturers (William J. Young & Sons, of Philadelphia) for the National Observatory at Washington City. The telescope is five feet six inches in length, and has an object-glass four inches in diameter. The two circles are each thirty inches in diameter. That used as a finder for the Transit reads with vernier to minutes. The Meridian Circle reads with four microscopes to two seconds of arc. It is furnished with a Collimation Micrometer, measuring to within six-tenths of a second of arc, and by estimation to six-hundredths of a second; with a level showing a change so small as to seven seconds of arc. An iron reversing stand serves not only for adjusting the instrument, but also as a safe carriage, to transfer it to the piers in the Prime Vertical room, in the North wing, where are duplicates of all the fixed mountings, the same instrument being used for both kinds of observations.

We have now considered all of the instruments, and their special uses. Let us ascend this short flight of steps from the Equatorial Room to the well-guarded flat roof, on which the students make wide observations of the heavens with unaided vision. To us, without teacher or instrument, and standing in this bright sunlight, we see nothing more interesting from this elevated point than a serene sky, a pleasant panorama of rural beauty, and the great College building and its dependencies.

Southward of us rises the Gymnasium, to which we

will now go, passing on the way the Steam and Gas house, seen a little in the distance in the picture of the Observatory, on page 146. It is three hundred and fifty feet east of the College building, and is used for generating materials for heating and lighting it. Four boilers, whose furnaces consume about fourteen hundred tons of coal in a year, send steam sufficient through an iron main to give to the entire College building a temperature not lower than sixty-five degrees Fahrenheit. From mains in its cellars, the steam is conveyed in felted pipes along the corridors of the first floor, from which go branches to every part of the building. In a similar manner gas is conveyed to and distributed through the building.

THE RIDING SCHOOL.

The Gymnasium is a spacious edifice on a gentle eminence, and contains rooms for a Riding School, Calisthenics, and Bowling Alley; a Music Hall, Stables, apartments for five families, and rooms for a variety of other purposes not connected with the main use of the building. It is irregular in form. Its greatest width is one hundred and thirty feet, and its entire depth one hundred and forty-five feet. The Riding School room is sixty by one hundred and twenty feet in area and forty-six feet in height, and is well lighted and ventilated. Herein the pupils are taught how to enjoy the pleasure and benefits of one of the most exhilarating modes of out-of-door exercise, which is too little practiced by women in all lands, and especially in our own. It is a new thing under the sun to have a riding-school a part of the instrumentalities of a seminary for the education of Young Women. In this, as in other things, Vassar College is a pioneer in a good work. It has been from the beginning an earnest desire of the Founder to have physical training a prominent feature of the institution, and every necessary provision has been made for that object.

The hall for the practice of Calisthenics is thirty feet in width and eighty feet in length, and is thoroughly equipped with every implement used in the system of Dr. Dio Lewis. Here, in appropriate and convenient costume, the pupils are instructed in the scientific use of their whole physical frame, in a manner that gives pleasure and tends to impart health and vigor to the system, and grace and ease to motion. We may not over-estimate the importance of this part of education, which is now being introduced into the best schools of our country. It is a hopeful revival of that ancient wisdom that gave to Phidias and Apelles models for their exquisite delineations (one in marble, the other on canvas) of the mother of Love of the old Greek mythology.

Gymnastic exercises seem to have been as old as the Greek nation itself, and they gave to the body that healthy and beautiful development by which they excelled all other nations, and imparted to their minds that power and elasticity which will ever be admired in all

THE CALISTHENIC HALL.

their productions. In the rapidly growing popularity of physical training of both sexes in this country, is a bright promise for the future strength of our people.

Physical exercise at Vassar College is not confined to in-door movements. There are opportunities for gardening on the broad domain. During hours of relaxation from study, knots of croquet-players may be seen at accustomed places. Horseback riding on the road is practiced; and strolls over the adjacent country, under the lead of tutors, in search of Geological or Botanical knowledge, or the obtaining of specimens of natural history, or for sketching from nature, are frequent in fine weather; while walking about the beautiful grounds,—growing more beautiful every day,—and rowing on Mill Cove Lake in Summer, and skating on its icy surface in Winter, make up the sum of exercise in open air. In the accompanying sketch, Professor Van Ingen has given us a pleasing picture of the out-of-door costume for riding, strolling, and croquet-playing of the first students of Vassar College.

COSTUME OF THE FIRST STUDENTS OF VASSAR COLLEGE.

We have lingered long in the buildings; but let us now go out and enjoy the fresh air, and the natural beauties of the College grounds, before re-entering the main edifice, and observing the arrangement, duties, and labors of the working force within it. We will pass out of this stately gateway (see page 109), almost a thousand feet from the College building, into the public road that separates the Campus from the Vegetable Garden westward of it. Its size is twenty-three by fifty-five feet, with a carriage-way of twenty-four feet. It includes a dwelling on each side, and is built of the same sort of materials, and in the same general style, as the College edifice.

Turn to the left, and follow this pleasant winding road down to Mill Cove Lake, a beautiful sheet of water on

Mill Cove Lake in Summer.

the College grounds, without an inlet, for it is supplied by springs. Along its margin, near the road, are some venerable and picturesque willow trees, scarred by age and tempests. On one side of the lake is a slope, fringed at the water's edge with shrubbery and rushes, and on the opposite side is a bank covered with evergreen and deciduous trees. The bosom of the tiny lake often presents scenes of great animation at all seasons. In the Summer it is dotted with boats, in which students are engaged in the healthful exercise of rowing, while at the little wharves of plank, groups of expectants are waiting their turn to enjoy the pleasure. In the Winter, when, as Job says, "the waters are hid as with a stone, and the face of the deep is frozen," the same students cover it with skaters. The water is always pellucid; always inflowing and outflowing; and never presents any evidence of stagnation.

On the opposite side of the road is the Pump-house (once a mill), the machinery in which sends twenty thousand gallons of pure water every day to the great tanks in the attic of the College edifice, and a sufficiency for use in the other buildings on the grounds. The water passes from the lake along an iron pipe into two immense filters, through which it percolates rapidly into a receiver. From this reservoir it is pumped through pipes, by either steam or water power, in a continually ascending stream, about

THE PUMP-HOUSE AND ITS SURROUNDINGS.

twenty-three hundred feet, and then into the tanks at the top of the College building, which have each a capacity of eight thousand gallons. Near the Pump-house is the Ice-house, whose treasures are gathered from the lake. A little distance from it are the farm stables and the farmer's dwelling-house, all of which are indicated on the map on page 99. We will go through this gate on the left, and follow the path down the hill to Mill Cove Brook, cross the bridge, and the bottom of the little grassy valley, to those double trees on the slope, where we shall have an interesting view of this group of buildings, and a glimpse of the lake beyond.

Turn now, and follow this pathway along the margin of the sweet little vale of Mill Cove Brook, which is traversed by the clear stream that might well be called Minnehaha, or laughing water. How beautiful are those green slopes, dotted with sturdy oaks, and here and there

SCENE IN THE VALLEY OF MILL COVE BROOK.

a maple or an elm! In the shadows of these trees, in warm June days, students may be seen walking, or studying, or sitting in groups, in pleasant interchange of thoughts of home and friends as the College year draws to a close, presenting an Arcadian scene in aspect; or at early morning they go down and gather wild flowers in the meadow on the margin of the brook, reminding one of Chaucer's fair Emilie, who

> "At every turn she took, and made a stand,
> And thrust among the thorns her little hand,
> To draw a flower; and every flower she drew,
> She shook the stalk and brushed away the dew;
> These parti-colored flowers of white and red
> She wove to make a garland for her head;
> This done, she sung and caroled out so clear,
> That men and angels might rejoice to hear."

GROVE OF ANCIENT WILLOWS.

Farther down the vale, where a dell, irrigated by a little stream, spreads out into a low, moist meadow, may be seen a charming subject for the painter of rural scenery. It is a grove of ancient willows, whose roots have been swayed in the oozy earth by the tempests among their branches, until the huge trunks stand leaning in picturesque confusion of outline. Near these the Mill Cove Brook runs cheerily by, and at the extremity of the College grounds, in this direction, commingles with another stream, that comes down from behind the Observatory and the foot of Sunset Hill. Where they meet, and form Caspar's Kil, is one of the most charming of the quiet places on the domain. There the half-wooded little hills approach each other, and the inwoven branches of the trees, with their covering of verdure, form a sheltering canopy for the bed of the wedded brooks. It is a spot beautiful as the Vale of Avoca; and in the hearts of many of the students of Vassar College who shall learn to

THE MEETING OF THE WATERS.

love each other, and shall "hold sweet counsel together" at this meeting of the waters, Memory will doubtless often, in after years, awaken the sentiment of Moore—

> "There is not in the wide world a valley so sweet,
> As that vale in whose bosom the bright waters meet:

Oh! the last rays of feeling and life must depart
Ere the bloom of that valley shall fade from the heart."

Now let us climb this slope of Sunset Hill to the summit. From this point we overlook the whole domain of the College possessions, and far around it. Yonder are

HEAD OF THE GLEN.

the spires of Poughkeepsie; but the beautiful city is almost hidden by intervening ridges. Looking in that general direction, you discern the pale blue line of the distant Shawangunk mountains, in which the bear, the deer, and the catamount abound. In the farther north, full forty miles distant, you see the lofty range of the Katsbergs (Catskill Mountains) melting into the rolling farm-lands of Albany County. As we turn slowly, the eye comprehends many a charming picture among the rugged hills and cultivated fields of Ulster and Orange Counties, along the line of the Hudson River, all the way to the Highlands, the unity broken only once or twice by hill-tops near. Here the students take delight in the visions of glowing sunsets; and in the early twilight they follow this broad path, that leads down to a bridge and up the hill by the Gymnasium to the College building.

We will turn to the right at the bridge, and go up the stream to the head of the Glen, where we shall be rewarded with a picture of wild beauty at a group of aged hemlocks, which stand by the side of the pathway that comes down to the brook from the ridge near the Observatory. Places like these the Poets people with Fairies at the twilight hour; but here the Prosaist discovers something better—

> "A Creature not too bright or good
> For human nature's daily food;
>
> . . . .
>
> A Being breathing thoughtful breath—
> A traveler between life and death;
>
> . . . .
>
> And yet a Spirit still, and bright
> With something of an Angel light."

Our ramble is ended. We will re-enter the College building, and observe the forces in operation under its roof.

The College work was commenced, as we have observed, on the 20th day of September, 1865, by a President, a Lady Principal, eight Professors, and twenty

Instructors and Teachers. These composed the force for government and instruction. The duties of the general management of the affairs of the institution were assigned to an Executive Committee, composed of seven members of the Board of Trustees; a Treasurer; a Secretary, who is also a general Superintendent; and a Registrar.

The special duties of Treasurer and Secretary are implied by their titles. In addition to the usual labors of a Secretary, that officer is required to superintend the general Business Department of the College, under the direction of the Executive Committee. He has charge of the farm, garden, grounds, boats, and all other property of the Institution; of all purchases, construction, repairs, and improvements; of the Steward, Matron, Janitor, Engineer, Farmer, and Gardener's Departments; and exercises a supervision over all the material and economic interests of the College, in these various departments. His duties are wide and various; and he is the chief organ of communication between the Executive Committee and those employed in the several departments of physical labor, who number about a hundred persons.

The Registrar is the accountant and general Clerk of the President, whose duty is to keep a register of all students admitted to the College; their places of residence, the names of their parents or guardians, and their post-office addresses. He has charge of the Depository of books and stationery; and he attends to receiving, forwarding, and delivering all mail matter and express packages, at the College. The officers of the Board of Trustees first appointed, and yet continued, are WILLIAM KELLY, *Chairman;* MATTHEW VASSAR, JR., *Treasurer;* and CYRUS SWAN, *Secretary.* JAMES N. SCHOU is *Registrar.*

The duties of the several officers are strictly defined. The President is the chief executive officer of the College, whose business is to execute all laws and regulations adopted by the Board of Trustees, or the Executive Committee, for the internal control of the Institution, and is responsible for his official acts to those two bodies only. This broad definition implies various and important special duties, all of which are enumerated and prescribed in a code of "Laws and Regulations of Vassar College."

The Lady Principal is the Chief Executive aid of the President in the direction of the teachers and in the government of the students. Her duties are many, delicate, and very important, and, under the established laws and rules of the Institution, she is immediately responsible to the President in the performance of them. To her is assigned the task of executing all the laws and regulations of the College relating to the conduct of the students when out of the class and lecture rooms. She exercises over them a maternal supervision in their private apartments (which she has the right of access to at all times), in the dining hall, in the corridors, in the public rooms and grounds of the College, and in their intercourse with the neighboring community. She is also required to use her best efforts to improve the personal habits, social training, and moral and religious culture of the students. As in the case of the President, this broad definition of her duties implies many special labors which the laws and regulations of the College prescribe. In like manner, the duties, privileges, and powers of the Professors are defined.

The Faculty consists of the President, Lady Principal,

and the Professors in the regular collegiate course, whose duty is to hold meetings at least once a week, at a time and place appointed by the President. The transactions at these meetings are both administrative and legislative, and pertain wholly to the business of government and instruction.

The Faculty are required, at the commencement of each year, to choose a Secretary to keep a record of all their official transactions, which shall be at all times open for the inspection of any member of the Faculty, of the Executive Committee, or of the Board of Trustees. Their transactions are all subject to the scrutiny and supervision of the Executive Committee, which meets regularly once in a fortnight, at the College office. Such is the administrative force of Vassar College.

While ample provision is made for the moral and intellectual culture of the students, equally ample provision is made for their bodily health and comfort. Their parlors and bedrooms, as we have observed, are in groups. Some of the chambers contain single, and others double beds, to suit the taste and circumstances of occupants. They are all airy and cheerful, opening on one side upon the College grounds, and on the other into the spacious corridors. The rooms are neatly carpeted and furnished, and are kept in order by the Matron. On each floor, at the center of the building, are bathing-rooms and water-closets, denoted on the plans by Roman numerals. A resident physician, in the person of the Professor of Physiology and Hygiene, and a well-equipped Infirmary, are provided for them in sickness; and in health they have the ample Gymnasium and the College grounds for in-door and out-of-door exercises of various kinds, for the promotion of physical vigor and mental strength. There are walks and drives on the College grounds, already completed, full three miles in extent, and the distance is continually increasing by laying out new courses. The purest spring water, filtered, is used for every purpose in the College, and the table is abundantly provided with a variety of the most wholesome food.

Applicants for admission to the College are required to be at least fifteen years of age, and to furnish satisfactory testimonials of character. Most of the students are received for the regular College course, but many are admitted to pursue special studies, selected by the advice and with the approval of the President. All must enter for the whole, or what remains, of the College year, and must pass a satisfactory examination in the ordinary English branches. Candidates for the first year of the regular course are examined to a certain extent in Latin, French, and Algebra. Those for an advanced standing in the regular course are examined in all the preceding studies; and special students, who desire to enter advanced classes in any Department, must be prepared in the preliminary branches of that Department.

The special classes are not open to all, indiscriminately, or at the mere option of the student or her friends; but only to those who can enter them consistently with sound principles of education. The regular course is designed for those who seek a thorough and liberal education, and extends through four years. Each department of instruction is placed under the responsible direction of a Professor, aided by the requisite number of teachers. More particular information concerning the Collegiate Departments, the subjects for instruction in each, and the textbooks and books of reference used, may be found in the Annual Catalogue of the College.

In the extra Collegiate Department there is a School of Vocal and Instrumental Music, and a School of Design. In the former, instruction is given partly in separate lessons to individuals, and partly to classes. The aim of all musical instruction in Vassar College is, as in other departments, in keeping with the expressed desire of its Founder, which is rather to create and develop a genuine love for all that is good and great in knowledge, and thereby cultivate the heart and discipline the mind of the student, than to spend precious time in the acquirement of expertness in mere recitation, performance, and execution. For the use of this School there are thirty music-rooms, and an equal number of pianos. The rudiments of musical theory are taught, and chorus-singing practiced in vocal classes, arranged according to proficiency, to which all the members of the College are admitted. Solo-singing, Organ-playing, and the higher branches of theory, Thorough-bass and Composition, are taught in private lessons exclusively.

Instructions in the School of Design cover the whole ground of Elementary Drawing and Painting, for which purpose the contents of the Art Gallery are freely used. The discipline and culture in this department, as of that of music, is most thorough. The student is carried through a carefully arranged progressive course, to which she is strictly confined; and in a large degree Nature furnishes her with models. She is educated in the essential principles of art, while training her eye and hand to its successful practice.

The testimony of competent observers now, at the close

of the second collegiate year, is, that in every Department of Vassar College there is evidence of the most faithful, enlightened, and efficient work; and that positive results are sufficiently manifest to entitle the institution to rank with the best seminaries of learning in the world. The College is empowered by its charter to confer all the usual and honorary academic degrees; and there seem to be, in the early achievements of the institution, promises that the time is not far distant when an honor conferred by Vassar College for Young Women will be as acceptable as that given by the older Colleges and Universities for Young Men.

The first collegiate year of Vassar College was an important one, for it was its formative period. Three hundred students were there at the beginning, and the number soon increased to over three hundred and fifty, of whom one hundred and fifteen of the younger were from fifteen to sixteen years of age, and fifty-four of the more mature were from twenty to twenty-four years of age. Every necessary article of equipment was ready for their service; and it seemed, to the superficial observer, that an easy task lay before the Faculty. Not so. They had to encounter a most difficult and laborious one. The perfect machinery was all there, but it needed the most careful adjustment and lubrication before it could be put into harmonious action; and wise, thoughtful, and assiduous efforts were required to make that adjustment. With surprising facility and success the Faculty proceeded in their delicate work, and it was not long before each instructor and student was laboring in proper order, and the friction of the great machine, considering its complexity, was very little.

The most difficult portion of the labor of organization necessarily devolved upon the President and Lady Principal. They were often compelled to plan without a precedent, in conformity to the law of circumstances; and most anxiously did they labor. In that work the duties of the Lady Principal were specially delicate and important, for she was to be the official Mother of the great Family so suddenly gathered, and composed of the most diverse elements, of the nature of which every thing had to be learned. Upon her devolved the duty of receiving students on their first arrival; of assigning them rooms and room-mates, and of providing the means of healthful social excitement. Upon her devolved the task of establishing a system, conforming as nearly as possible to the most perfect family plan, for the domestic and social life of the College, that should allow the greatest possible individual action and development, and at the same time exercise all needful control. The great question presented itself: How shall we individualize the students so as to guard against the evils incident to so large an assemblage of immature young people, and to impress upon the mind of each, without a galling *espionage*, the conviction that she is thoroughly known and hourly cared for?

This important question was promptly met with a practical solution, the wisdom of which is confirmed by all subsequent experience. When the Spring of 1866 came, and six months of labor and trial had passed, Vassar College, in its material, intellectual, social, and religious aspect, presented the most gratifying assurance of its abundant success. Flourishing Literary Societies had been formed among the students for their mutual improvement, and the pursuit of knowledge was, to most of them, a pleasure and not a task—a privilege and not a duty.

The value of Vassar College was now appreciated by the students, and they felt a strong desire to manifest, collectively, their gratitude to the Founder, whose munificence had offered to their sex so many blessings. The opportunity was nigh. The College Faculty had just resolved, "That the 29th of April, the anniversary of the birthday of Matthew Vassar, Founder of this College, be, and hereby is, entered on its Calendar as a holiday, to be annually observed by commemorative exercises; and that this anniversary be designated 'The Founder's Day.'" This resolution offered the coveted opportunity, and the students were permitted to make their desired demonstration on "The Founder's Day."

It was resolved by the students to give the Founder a public reception at the College on that, his seventy-fourth birthday, in the presence of friends, and with appropriate literary exercises. Every heart was interested, and every finger was made busy in the work of love. All was in readiness at the appointed time. The day was perfect in serenity and temperature. The invited guests were assembled in the College parlors at five o'clock in the evening. At that hour there was no outward token of any thing unusual, excepting a beautiful triumphal arch, covered with evergreens, which had been raised over the broad avenue leading from the Porter's Lodge to the College. On it were the words, "WELCOME TO THE FOUNDER." In the center was his monogram, gracefully arranged. On one side was the date of his birth, "APRIL 29, 1792;" and on the other side the date of the celebration, "APRIL 29, 1866." Over all fluttered gay flags and banners.

The Founder had received no intimation of the intended honor. The President called at his house in the city that afternoon, invited him to ride out to the College at about six o'clock in the evening, and offered to accompany him. In this act there was nothing remarkable. The time of the short journey was spent in ordinary conversation, and the Founder had no suspicions of what he was to experience when his carriage should reach the Porter's Lodge. There he beheld a sight sufficiently strange and beautiful to make him doubt the testimony of his own eyes.

One of the students, acting as Marshal, and accompanied by two aids, had led her fellow-students in two columns toward the Porter's Lodge, and halted in a position to form a continuous line on each side of the avenue, from the gateway to the circle in front of the main entrance to the College. They were neatly arrayed in garments of almost every variety of color, and presented a spectacle of rare beauty and interest. When the carriage of the Founder, in which were only himself and the President, passed into the avenue, he was greeted with the waving of white handkerchiefs and the smiles of a host of delighted students. The heads of the two columns then turned, and, countermarching, formed a flanking escort for the carriage and a long procession. Meanwhile the Faculty and Teachers were waiting near the entrance to the College; and, when the venerable and venerated man alighted from his carriage, a glad song of welcome burst from the lips of a selected choir on the portico, standing under flags and evergreens that decorated the front of the building. Tears were the only expression of gratitude which the Founder could then give in response, for deep emotion had sealed his lips.

Supported by the President, Mr. Vassar now entered the College vestibule, and was conducted by the Marshal and her aids to a private parlor, where he was introduced to the President of the day, and by her presented to others. The company then repaired to the Chapel, which was tastefully decorated with evergreens and flowers. Over the portrait of the Founder were the words, in illuminated letters on a white ground, THE DESIRE ACCOMPLISHED IS SWEET TO THE SOUL. When the Trustees of the College and the students and guests were seated, Mr. Vassar, surrounded by the Faculty and his feminine escort, entered the door. Then the organ pealed forth a stirring voluntary, and the whole audience arose and remained standing until the Chief Guest was seated. The President of the College then offered a prayer. It was followed by music from a piano by one of the students, and the literary exercises proper began by a Salutatory, in which, in chaste and glowing language, all the guests were welcomed.

An essay on "The World's Advance" was now read. This was followed by music and recitations, concerning Woman's social position in different periods of the world. The students engaged in this well-arranged performance appeared in appropriate costume—one as Deborah, another as Xantippe, a third as Joan of Arc, and so on. After this came music, and then the reading of a delightful poem, entitled "Hilltop Idyl." This, like every other composition on the occasion, was an original production of the student by whom it was read or recited. It was followed by a "Floral Tribute," which presented a beautiful spectacle. Then one, in the character of a "Representative Student," read the following "Address to the Founder:"—

"Beloved and honored sire!
We come with flowers,
To speak for us words passing our weak speech.
List! how their fragrant hearts breathe redolent
Our grateful wishes for thy natal day.
They are Spring's firstlings—rich in promises;
So greeteth thee to-day the first glad springing
Of what thine hands have planted;
Long Summer years shall come with bloom and fruitage.
This crown of flowers
We give thee in the name of womanhood,
Whom thou hast crowned;
These flowers are earthly—fading—
May He, who smiles even here on high emprise,
And noble deed, wrought humbly in His name,
Place on thy brow at last the unfading crown
Of immortelles that angels gather."

A large choir, accompanied by the organ, closed the exercises in the Chapel by singing an original song, entitled "Our Father and Friend," when the whole audience arose and joined in chanting the Doxology. Then all repaired to the Dining Hall, where the students had provided a bountiful collation; and the remainder of the evening was spent in the parlors and corridors, in pleasant social intercourse.

Here we will leave Vassar College and its Founder to the tender consideration of Posterity, for whose good they exist. In all future ages, the name of Matthew Vassar will be found conspicuous among those of the benefactors of his race. The heralds of that glorious fame came thickly when intelligence of his great act went abroad, all speaking in language similar to one whose whole communication was—"In Heaven Angels sing God's praise—on

Earth Women and all good Men sing yours. Long may you live to hear it, is the prayer of a Stranger."

That "prayer of a Stranger" has been answered. Mr. Vassar has lived to hear the just plaudits of his fellow-men. He has lived to see his great work accomplished. He has lived to participate in the second celebration of "The Founder's Day," crowned with the blessings of good health and cheerfulness of spirit. He has lived to enjoy the fruition of his labors in a great work of benevolence. With his own hand he planted, in generous soil, the seed of a tree whose fruit shall be for the moral healing of the nations. With his own hand he fostered the tender germ, and cultivated the growing sapling, until now he sees it in maturity of form and strength, and laden with abundant blossoms, that prophecy of rich harvests of blessings throughout many generations.

www.ingramcontent.com/pod-product-compliance
Lightning Source LLC
LaVergne TN
LVHW011236110826
845150LV00006B/1653

9781425514136